PUBLIC SECTOR DEFICITS IN OECD COUNTRIES

Public Sector Deficits in OECD Countries

Causes, Consequences and Remedies

Edited by
Henry Cavanna
Executive Director, Fondation Internationale des Sciences Humaines, Paris

M
MACMILLAN
PRESS

First published 1988

Published by
THE MACMILLAN PRESS LTD
Houndmills, Basingstoke, Hampshire RG21 2XS
and London
Companies and representatives
throughout the world

Printed in Hong Kong

British Library Cataloguing in Publication Data
Public sector deficits in OECD countries:
causes, consequences and remedies
1. Budget deficits
I. Cavanna, Henry
346.3′43317′7 HJ2005
ISBN 0–333–42308–9

Contents

Notes on the Contributors

Henry Cavanna
Executive Director, Fondation Internationale des Sciences Humaines, Paris

Jean-Claude Chouraqui
Head of the Monetary and Budgetary Policies Division OECD

Terenzio Cozzi
Professor of Economics, the University of Turin

Walter Eltis
Lecturer in Economics and Fellow of Exeter College, Oxford University and, since 1986, Economic Director of The National Economic Development Office, London

*Rudolph G. Penner**
Director of the Congressional Budget Office, the Congress of the United States

Dominique Strauss-Kahn
Professor of Economics, University of Paris-Dauphine

Manfred Willms
Director of the Institute for Economic Policy, the University of Kiel

* The paper on The Consequences of Persistent Large Budget Deficits was prepared by the Congress Budget Office staff, working under the direction of Mr Rudolph Penner.

Introduction

For many years in the postwar era, debts grew at the same rate as the economy. The ratio between debt and GNP remained at a remarkably steady 1.4–1. But from around 1981–82, something seems to have happened to that relationship, as E. Gerald Corrigan, President of the Federal Reserve Bank of New York, reminded us recently.

From 1981–85 the ratio of debt to GNP has risen about 20 base points, 'a very large change in a ratio of this nature'. An extrapolation of the recent trade suggests, wrote T. B. Clark recently, that by 1995 the United States would have $2.25 debt for every dollar of economic output. These figures speak for themselves.

Though the United States has perhaps led the way as a debtor, the situation of other Western countries' economies also gives cause for concern.

The papers published here deal mainly with Public Sector Deficits in OECD countries. They state the causes of those deficits and their consequences and they point out remedies. After an overview of the situation in OECD countries by Jean-Claude Chouraqui, the contributors write about their own countries: the USA – Rudolph G. Penner; the United Kingdom – Walter Eltis; Germany – Manfred Willms; Italy – Terenzio Cozzi; and France – Dominique Strauss-Kahn.

This collection is, I believe, a sober and serious assessment, made by world-renowned experts, of a most relevant topic.

Henry Cavanna

Editor's Note

I wish especially to thank Mr Rudolph G. Penner for permission to reprint here 'The Consequences of Persistent Large Budget Deficits', published in '*The Economic and Budget Outlook: Fiscal Years 1986–1990*' (Congressional Budget Office of the United States).

All other papers were presented and discussed at the International Symposium on Public Deficits held in Madrid in February 1985. The Conference was organised by the Fondation Internationale des Sciences Humaines, Paris, and the Fundacion Fondo Investigacion Economica y Social, Madrid.

1 Public Sector Deficits in OECD Countries: Causes, Consequences and Policy Reaction*

Jean-Claude Chouraqui

Most of the OECD Member countries experienced a significant increase in their public sector deficits during the years following the first oil shock of 1973. The measures adopted shortly after, in order to bring these deficits back down to levels comparable to those observed in the past, have been only partially successful and the consequences of the second oil shock, which occurred in 1979, have contributed to aggravate the problem (see Table 1.1).

This trend coincided with a rapid growth of the public sector, which was characterised by the following features:

- an increase in public expenditure and taxation as a proportion of GDP (see Table 1.2);
- a rise in the share of current transfer payments in public spending, which, combined with the growth of employment in public services, has resulted in an increase in incomes distributed by the public sector (in the form of salaries and transfer payments) as a proportion of total national income;
- an increase in the share of consumption spending in total government expenditure and a corresponding fall in the proportion of resources allocated to public investment.

In view of the fact that any continuation of such tendencies could have adverse consequences for resource allocation, and therefore for

*This article is in part a summary of some of the arguments set out in various recent OECD publications. These publications are quoted in the notes to the text. The views expressed therein, however, are those of the author and do not necessarily reflect the opinions of the OECD or of its Member countries. The author would like to thank Sylvie Toly for her help in the preparation of the statistical tables.

TABLE 1.1 *Actual budget balances: General government financial surplus or deficit (−) as a percentage of nominal GNP*[a]

	1970	*1971*	*1972*	*1973*	*1974*	*1975*	*1976*	*1977*	*1978*	*1979*	*1980*	*1981*	*1982*	*1983*	*1984*	*1985*[b]
United States	−1.1	−1.8	−0.3	0.6	−0.3	−4.2	−2.1	−0.9	0.2	0.6	−1.2	−0.9	−3.8	−4.1	−3.4	−3.9
Japan	1.8	1.2	−0.1	0.6	0.4	−2.7	−3.7	−3.8	−5.5	−4.8	−4.5	−4.0	−3.6	−3.5	−2.7	−1.7
Germany	0.2	−0.2	−0.5	1.2	−1.3	−5.7	−3.4	−2.4	−2.5	−2.6	−2.9	−3.7	−3.3	−2.5	−1.9	−1.2
France	0.9	0.7	0.8	0.9	0.6	−2.2	−0.5	−0.8	−1.9	−0.7	0.2	−1.8	−2.7	−3.1	−2.8	−3.3
United Kingdom	2.4	1.4	−1.8	−3.4	−3.8	−4.7	−4.9	−3.4	−4.2	−3.5	−3.5	−2.8	−2.3	−3.7	−3.8	−3.4
Italy	−5.0	−7.1	−9.2	−8.5	−8.1	−11.7	−9.0	−8.0	−9.7	−9.5	−8.0	−11.9	−12.6	−12.4	−13.5	−13.4
Canada	0.9	0.1	0.1	1.0	1.9	−2.4	−1.7	−2.4	−3.1	−1.8	−2.7	−1.6	−5.0	−6.2	−6.3	−6.5
Total for major seven countries[c]	−0.2	−0.9	−0.8	−0.1	−0.8	−4.3	−2.9	−2.2	−2.2	−1.7	−2.4	−2.5	−4.0	−4.2	−3.8	−3.8
Australia	2.9	2.4	2.2	−0.2	2.4	−0.6	−3.0	−0.7	−2.2	−2.2	−1.3	−0.2	0.0	−3.8	−3.2	−2.9
Austria	1.0	1.5	2.0	1.3	1.3	−2.5	−3.7	−2.4	−2.8	−2.4	−1.7	−1.7	−3.2	−3.8	−2.3	−2.2
Belgium	−2.0	−3.0	−4.0	−3.5	−2.6	−4.7	−5.4	−5.5	−6.0	−6.5	−8.4	−14.2	−12.5	−13.3	−11.3	−10.0
Denmark	3.2	3.9	3.9	5.2	3.1	−1.4	−0.3	−0.6	−0.3	−1.7	−3.3	−6.9	−9.1	−7.3	−4.3	−2.4
Finland	4.4	4.6	3.9	5.8	4.7	2.7	4.8	3.2	1.4	0.5	0.5	1.3	−0.4	−1.6	0.2	0.7

Greece	−0.1	−0.9	−0.3	−1.4	−2.2	−3.4	−2.6	−2.1	−1.7	−2.4	−2.7	−11.9	−7.3	−9.4	−10.3	−11.6
Netherlands	−0.8	−0.5	−0.6	0.6	−0.4	−3.0	−2.9	−2.1	−3.1	−3.7	−4.2	−5.6	−7.2	−6.6	−6.4	−5.3
Norway	3.2	4.3	4.5	5.7	4.7	3.8	3.1	1.7	0.6	3.4	5.7	4.7	4.4	3.8	6.2	5.2
Spain	0.7	−0.6	0.3	1.1	0.2	0.0	−0.3	−0.6	−1.8	−1.8	−2.0	−3.0	−5.3	−5.3	−5.0	−4.8
Sweden	4.4	5.2	4.4	4.1	2.0	2.8	4.5	1.7	−0.5	−2.9	−3.7	−4.9	−6.1	−5.1	−3.3	−2.4
Total for smaller countries[c]	1.4	1.2	1.2	1.3	0.9	−0.9	−1.1	−1.0	−2.1	−2.5	−2.6	−4.1	−4.9	−5.5	−4.4	−4.0
Total for above countries[c]	0.1	−0.6	−0.5	0.1	−0.6	−3.9	−2.7	−2.0	−2.2	−1.8	−2.4	−2.7	−4.1	−4.4	−3.9	−3.8
Total excluding United States	0.8	0.2	−0.7	−0.3	−0.8	−3.6	−3.1	−2.8	−3.9	−3.5	−3.3	−4.0	−4.4	−4.7	−4.2	−3.8

a. On an SNA basis, except for the United States, the United Kingdom, Greece and the Netherlands for which figures are based on national income statistics.
b. OECD estimates.
c. 1982 GNP weights and exchange rates.

SOURCE: OECD.

TABLE 1.2A *Trends in general government taxation and expenditure: United States; as a percentage of nominal GNP*

	1970	1971	1972	1973	1974	1975	1976	1977	1978	1979	1980	1981	1982	1983	1984	1985[a]
TAX RECEIPTS																
Direct taxes	15.1	14.3	15.4	15.1	15.5	14.1	15.2	15.6	15.8	16.1	16.0	15.9	15.1	14.5	14.3	14.3
Indirect taxes	9.5	9.6	9.4	9.1	9.0	9.0	8.8	8.6	8.2	7.8	8.1	8.5	8.4	8.5	8.3	8.4
Social Security	5.9	6.0	6.3	7.0	7.3	7.1	7.3	7.3	7.5	7.7	7.7	8.0	8.2	8.3	8.4	8.7
Current receipts total																
1. Actual	30.5	29.9	31.1	31.1	31.7	30.2	31.4	31.6	31.5	31.6	31.8	32.3	31.8	31.3	31.0	31.4
2. Cyclically adjusted[b]	30.7	29.9	31.1	31.1	31.8	30.2	31.4	31.6	31.5	31.6	31.8	32.3	31.4	30.9	31.0	31.3
PUBLIC EXPENDITURE																
Government consumption on goods and services[c]	22.2	21.8	21.3	20.4	21.2	21.8	21.1	20.5	20.0	19.6	20.4	20.2	21.2	20.7	20.4	21.2
Current transfers	7.9	8.6	8.6	8.8	9.7	11.2	11.0	10.6	10.1	10.1	11.1	11.2	12.0	12.0	11.1	11.1
of which: social security	7.9	8.6	8.6	8.8	9.7	11.2	11.0	10.6	10.1	10.1	11.1	11.2	12.0	12.0	11.1	11.1

Interest on public debt	1.2	1.1	1.0	1.1	1.1	1.2	1.3	1.3	1.1	1.2	1.3	1.7	2.0	2.1	2.4	2.6
Current expenditure total	31.6	31.7	31.3	30.6	32.1	34.4	33.5	32.5	31.3	31.0	33.0	33.3	35.5	35.3	34.3	35.2
Total spending[d]																
1. Actual	31.6	31.7	31.3	30.6	32.1	34.4	33.5	32.5	31.3	31.0	33.0	33.3	35.5	35.3	34.3	35.2
2. Cyclically adjusted[b]	30.6	30.5	31.1	31.3	31.1	31.1	31.0	31.0	30.6	30.4	31.1	31.3	31.3	31.5	32.3	33.0

a. OECD estimates.
b. As a percentage of potential GNP.
c. Including investment, according to the definition of US national accounts.
d. As subsidies are not shown on the expenditure side, components do not add to the total.

SOURCE: OECD.

TABLE 1.2B *Trends in general government taxation and expenditure: other OECD countries*[a] *as a percentage of nominal GNP*

	1970	*1971*	*1972*	*1973*	*1974*	*1975*	*1976*	*1977*	*1978*	*1979*	*1980*	*1981*	*1982*	*1983*	*1984*	*1985*[b]
TAX RECEIPTS																
Direct taxes	10.1	10.3	10.2	10.7	11.8	11.5	11.6	11.8	11.7	11.8	12.4	12.7	13.0	13.0	13.2	13.4
Indirect taxes	11.8	11.8	11.7	11.5	11.2	10.9	11.1	11.3	11.3	11.6	11.8	12.0	12.1	12.1	12.2	12.2
Social Security	8.2	8.5	8.7	8.9	9.4	10.3	10.6	10.8	10.9	11.0	11.3	11.6	11.9	12.2	12.2	12.2
Current receipts total[c]																
1. Actual	32.6	33.2	33.0	33.6	35.1	35.5	36.1	36.9	36.8	37.4	38.6	39.8	40.6	40.9	41.3	41.5
1. Cyclically adjusted[d]	32.7	33.0	32.9	33.6	35.0	35.0	35.9	36.6	36.6	37.3	38.2	39.1	39.8	40.2	40.9	41.1
PUBLIC EXPENDITURE																
Government consumption on goods and services	13.4	13.9	14.1	14.1	14.9	16.0	15.9	15.9	16.0	15.9	16.3	16.8	17.0	17.1	16.9	16.7
Current transfers	10.8	11.2	11.8	11.8	12.5	14.0	14.4	14.7	15.4	15.4	15.6	16.5	17.2	17.6	17.5	17.5
of which: social security	10.1	10.4	10.8	10.9	11.6	13.0	13.4	13.5	14.0	14.0	14.3	15.1	15.8	16.1	15.9	16.0

Interest on public debt	1.7	1.7	1.7	1.8	1.9	2.1	2.4	2.6	2.8	3.0	3.3	3.8	4.3	4.6	4.8	5.0
Current expenditure total[c]	27.4	28.3	29.1	29.3	31.4	34.3	34.7	35.4	36.3	36.4	37.4	39.3	40.7	41.3	41.4	41.4
Gross investment	4.3	4.4	4.4	4.3	4.3	4.4	4.0	4.0	4.0	4.1	4.1	4.0	3.9	3.8	3.6	3.4
Total spending[c]																
1. Actual	31.8	32.9	33.7	33.9	35.9	39.1	39.2	39.7	40.7	40.9	41.9	43.8	45.0	45.5	45.5	45.3
2. Cyclically adjusted[d]	31.9	32.6	33.3	34.3	35.7	37.5	38.3	38.6	39.8	40.3	41.0	42.0	42.3	42.5	42.9	42.8

a. Average for the six major countries other than the United States and the eleven smaller countries indicated in Table 1.1, at 1982 GNP weights and exchange rates.
b. OECD estimates.
c. Components do not add to the total. Public entrepreneurial and property income are not shown on the receipts side, and nor are subsidies and net capital transfers on the expenditure side.
d. As a percentage of potential GNP.

SOURCE: OECD.

medium-term growth and inflation, governments have attempted to reverse them, with particular emphasis on the restructuring of public spending. Reducing the public sector's share of total expenditure as well as of overall capital market borrowings has thus become a priority for a large number of OECD countries.

The analysis below is intended to give an insight into the present situation as regards the task of controlling public sector deficits. Four aspects of the topic are dealt with, namely the origins of the deficits, their effects on economic activity, the link between deficits, monetary expansion and inflation and the policies that have been adopted with a view to reducing deficits.[1]

1.1 THE CAUSES OF PUBLIC SECTOR DEFICITS

Four main factors may be identified as responsible for the increase and persistence of public sector deficits:

- the effects of the slowdown in economic growth due to the 'automatic budget stabilisers';
- the growth of government debt interest payments;
- the effects of inflation on public spending through the 'fiscal indexation' mechanisms;
- the measures adopted by the authorities with a view to sustaining economic activity and employment.

Cyclical Effects

Shortly after the second oil shock, the OECD economies experienced a much sharper and longer slowdown in activity than initially foreseen. This led to a fall in tax receipts and increased transfer payments related to the rise in unemployment. Such effects are due to what are usually called 'automatic stabilisers', the slowdown in economic growth being reflected in a spontaneous expansion of the budget deficit.

Table 1.3 gives some indication of the impact of these automatic stabilisers on the growth of government deficits in the OECD area between 1971 and 1985. For this purpose, changes in actual budget balances (as indicated in Table 1.1) have been divided into those resulting from the cyclical economic situation – which represent the effect of the automatic stabilisers – and those of a structural nature, reflecting discretionary actions by government.[2] This comes down to calculating what the OECD countries budget balance would have been if economic growth had been in line with potential output corresponding to a high level of employment. The result is a cyclically adjusted (or 'structural') budget balance, the changes in which are given in the third line of Table 1.3. The automatic growth in public sector deficits as a result of the slowdown in economic activity and the rise in unemployment is indicated in the second line. As potential production has been extrapolated on the basis of the figures for 1971–72, the table shows that the automatic stabilisers contributed slightly more than two points to the change in budget balances during the period 1971 to 1985. This means that a return to a high level of employment, comparable to the situation at the beginning of the 1970s, would imply a proportionate improvement in the overall budget balance of the OECD countries. This is true of most of the countries under consideration, though to a lesser extent in Japan than elsewhere.

Another way of assessing the effects of cyclical factors on public sector deficits consists of looking at the *levels* of structural budget balances as a percentage of GDP.[3] These are given in Table 1.4 which shows that, between 1979 and 1985, the structural component of budget deficits in the OECD area as a whole remained stable at around 1.5 per cent of GDP. It would therefore appear that almost all of the increase (about 2 per cent of GDP) in actual deficits recorded during the same period should be attributed to the slowdown in economic activity.

To the extent, however, that the rise in the level of unemployment is due not simply to the slowdown in activity but is explicable also in terms of structural factors – such as demographic trends and labour market rigidities – public sector deficits may be considered to be partly structural in nature and likely to persist, rather than a temporary phenomenon associated with the short-term economic situation. In addition, it is possible that fiscal policy, by perhaps creating distortions in the supply of and the demand for labour (through the growth of unemployment benefits), has tended to increase under-employment, thereby helping to enhance the structural aspect of public sector deficits.[4] Although empirical studies are not conclusive in this respect,[5] it should be noted that the ratio of social security payments to gross domestic product has been following a distinctly rising trend in most OECD countries since the beginning of the 1970s (see Table 1.2).

TABLE 1.3 *Changes in cyclical and structural general government budget balances*[a], *as a percentage of nominal GNP*

	1971	*1972*	*1973*	*1974*	*1975*	*1976*	*1977*	*1978*	*1979*	*1980*	*1981*	*1982*	*1983*	*1984*	*1985*	*Total change 1971–85*
UNITED STATES																
1. Change in actual balance[b]	−0.7	1.5	0.9	−0.9	−3.9	2.1	1.2	1.1	0.4	−1.8	0.3	−2.8	−0.3	0.7	−0.5	−2.8
2. Change due to cyclical movements in activity[c]	−0.2	1.0	1.1	−1.8	−2.3	0.8	1.0	0.8	0.1	−1.3	−0.1	−1.9	0.4	1.4	−0.2	−1.1
3. Change in structural balance[d]	−0.5	0.5	−0.2	0.9	−1.6	1.3	0.2	0.3	0.3	−0.5	0.4	−0.9	−0.7	−0.7	−0.3	−1.7
4. Change in inflation-adjusted structural balance[e]	−1.1	0.2	0.4	1.6	−1.9	0.7	0.3	0.4	0.7	−0.3	−0.1	−1.5	−1.0	−0.7	−0.3	−2.7
JAPAN																
1. Change in actual balance[b]	−0.6	−1.3	0.7	−0.2	−3.1	−1.0	−0.1	−1.7	0.7	0.3	0.5	0.4	0.1	0.9	1.0	−3.5
2. Change due to cyclical movements in activity[c]	−0.4	0.2	0.4	−0.6	−0.5	0.1	0.1	0.1	0.0	−0.1	0.1	0.0	−0.5	0.3	0.2	−0.6
3. Change in structural balance[d]	−0.2	−1.5	0.3	0.4	−2.6	−1.1	−0.2	−1.8	0.7	0.4	0.4	0.3	0.6	0.5	0.8	−2.9
4. Change in inflation-adjusted structural balance[e]	−0.1	−1.4	−0.2	−0.1	−1.8	−0.6	0.1	−1.8	0.9	1.2	0.1	0.0	0.4	0.7	0.9	−1.7
GERMANY																
1. Change in actual balance[b]	−0.4	−0.3	1.7	−2.5	−4.4	2.3	1.0	−0.1	−0.1	−0.3	−0.8	0.4	0.8	0.5	0.8	−1.4
2. Change due to cyclical movements in activity[c]	−0.3	−0.5	0.4	−0.9	−1.5	1.0	0.1	0.3	0.5	0.0	−0.5	−0.8	−0.5	0.0	0.2	−2.4

3. Change in structural balance[d]	−0.1	0.2	1.3	−1.6	−2.9	1.3	0.9	−0.4	−0.6	−0.3	−0.3	1.2	1.3	0.5	0.5	1.0
4. Change in inflation-adjusted structural balance[e]	−0.2	0.2	1.3	−1.6	−2.6	1.5	1.0	−0.4	−0.4	−0.1	−0.1	1.2	1.1	0.4	0.5	1.7
FRANCE																
1. Change in actual balance[b]	−0.2	0.1	0.1	−0.3	−2.8	1.7	−0.3	−1.1	1.2	0.9	−2.0	−0.9	−0.3	0.3	−0.5	−4.2
2. Change due to cyclical movements in activity[c]	0.0	0.4	0.1	−0.6	−1.7	1.1	0.1	0.5	0.3	−0.4	−1.0	−0.4	−0.6	−0.9	−0.5	−3.6
3. Change in structural balance[d]	−0.2	−0.3	0.0	0.3	−1.1	0.6	−0.4	−1.6	0.9	1.3	−1.0	−0.6	0.2	1.2	0.0	−0.6
4. Change in inflation-adjusted structural balance[e]	−0.3	−0.2	0.0	0.8	−1.2	0.6	−0.5	−1.6	1.0	1.5	−1.0	−0.6	0.1	1.0	−0.1	−0.4
UNITED KINGDOM																
1. Change in actual balance[b]	−1.0	−3.2	−1.6	−0.4	−0.9	−0.2	1.5	−0.8	0.7	0.0	0.7	0.5	−1.4	−0.1	0.4	−5.8
2. Change due to cyclical movements in activity[c]	0.2	0.0	1.2	−1.3	−1.0	0.2	0.0	1.2	−0.1	−1.1	−2.1	−1.0	−0.1	0.3	0.2	−3.4
3. Change in structural balance[d]	−1.2	−3.2	−2.8	0.9	0.1	−0.4	1.5	−2.0	0.8	1.1	2.8	1.5	−1.3	−0.4	0.2	−2.4
4. Change in inflation-adjusted structural balance[e]	0.1	−4.8	−1.9	3.5	3.1	−3.1	1.2	−5.5	2.8	2.3	0.4	0.2	−2.6	−0.4	0.2	−4.4
ITALY																
1. Change in actual balance[b]	−2.1	−2.1	0.7	0.4	−3.6	2.7	1.0	−1.7	0.2	1.5	−3.9	−0.7	0.2	−1.2	0.1	−8.4
2. Change due to cyclical movements in activity[c]	−0.6	−0.4	0.6	0.2	−1.6	1.0	−0.1	0.1	0.7	0.6	−0.1	−1.2	−1.5	−1.0	0.0	−3.2

continued on page 12

Table 1.3 continued

	1971	1972	1973	1974	1975	1976	1977	1978	1979	1980	1981	1982	1983	1984	1985	Total change 1971–85
3. Change in structural balance[d]	−1.5	−1.7	0.1	0.2	−2.0	1.7	1.1	−1.8	−0.5	0.9	−3.8	0.6	1.7	−0.2	0.1	−5.2
4. Change in inflation-adjusted structural balance[e]	−1.3	−1.2	2.5	4.3	−2.6	2.2	2.1	−4.9	1.4	4.2	−5.0	−0.2	1.9	−2.0	−0.4	1.1
CANADA																
1. Change in actual balance[b]	−0.8	0.0	0.9	0.9	−4.3	0.7	−0.7	−0.7	1.3	−0.9	1.1	−3.4	−1.2	−0.2	−0.2	−7.4
2. Change due to cyclical movements in activity[c]	0.4	0.2	0.6	0.0	−0.8	0.5	−0.7	−0.1	0.1	−0.4	0.3	−3.0	0.5	0.8	0.7	−0.9
3. Change in structural balance[d]	−1.2	−0.2	0.3	0.9	−3.5	0.2	0.0	−0.6	1.2	−0.5	0.8	−0.4	−1.7	−1.0	−0.9	−6.5
4. Change in inflation-adjusted structural balance[e]	−1.8	−0.6	0.3	0.7	−3.5	0.3	−0.1	−0.5	1.5	−0.4	0.8	−0.3	−1.6	−0.9	−0.7	−6.9
TOTAL FOR SEVEN MAJOR COUNTRIES[f]																
1. Change in actual balance[b]	−0.7	0.1	0.7	−0.7	−3.5	1.4	0.7	0.0	0.5	−0.7	−0.1	−1.5	−0.2	0.5	0.0	−3.6
2. Change due to cyclical movements in activity[c]	−0.5	−0.4	−0.1	0.5	−1.8	0.7	0.3	−0.6	0.3	0.0	0.2	−1.3	0.0	0.7	0.0	−2.0
3. Change in structural balance[d]	−0.2	0.5	0.8	−1.2	−1.7	0.7	0.5	0.6	0.1	−0.7	−0.3	−0.2	−0.2	−0.2	0.0	−1.6
4. Change in inflation-adjusted structural balance[e]	−0.7	−0.6	0.3	1.2	−1.6	0.3	0.4	−0.9	0.8	0.6	−0.3	−0.6	−0.5	−0.3	0.0	−2.0

TOTAL FOR SMALLER COUNTRIES INDICATED IN TABLE 1.1[f]																
1. Change in actual balance[b]	−0.2	0.0	0.1	−0.3	−1.9	−0.2	0.1	−1.1	−0.4	−0.1	−1.5	−0.8	−0.6	1.1	0.5	−5.4
2. Change due to cyclical movements in activity[c]	0.0	−0.3	−0.5	−0.2	−0.7	−0.5	0.8	−0.7	−0.8	−0.3	−0.5	−0.7	−0.2	0.6	0.3	−3.7
3. Change in structural balance[d]	−0.2	0.3	0.6	−0.2	−1.1	0.4	−0.8	−0.4	0.5	0.1	−0.9	−0.1	−0.4	0.4	0.1	−1.7
4. Change in inflation-adjusted structural balance[e]		−0.3	−0.3	0.2	−0.7	−0.9	0.5	−1.0	−0.5	0.1	−0.3	0.1	−0.7	0.5	0.0	−3.3[g]
TOTAL FOR ABOVE COUNTRIES[f]																
1. Change in actual balance[b]	−0.6	0.1	0.6	−0.7	−3.3	1.2	0.7	−0.2	0.4	−0.6	−0.3	−1.4	−0.3	0.5	0.0	−3.8
2. Change due to cyclical movements in activity[c]	−0.5	−0.3	−0.2	0.4	−1.7	0.6	0.3	−0.6	0.2	0.0	0.1	−1.2	−0.1	0.7	0.0	−2.2
3. Change in structural balance[d]	−0.2	0.4	0.8	−1.1	−1.6	0.7	0.3	0.4	0.2	−0.6	−0.4	−0.2	−0.2	−0.1	0.0	−1.7
4. Change in inflation-adjusted structural balance[e]		−0.6	0.2	1.1	−1.5	0.2	0.4	−1.0	0.7	0.5	−0.3	−0.5	−0.5	−0.2	0.0	−1.6[g]

a. A positive value indicates a move towards restriction (surplus); a negative value indicates expansion (deficit). A positive value therefore reflects public expenditure cuts and tax increases.
b. Year-to-year changes in financial balances shown in Table 1.1.
c. 'Built-in stabilisers', estimated as the reaction of the budget deficit to variations in real GNP around the trend growth of productive potential.
d. Changes in cyclically adjusted budget balances as shown in Table 1.4. These reflect both deliberate policy action and fiscal drag.
e. Adjusted for the impact of price increases on net outstanding government debt.
f. 1982 GNP weighted.
g. Change over the period 1972–85.

SOURCE: OECD.

TABLE 1.4 *Structural budget balances: general government financial surplus or deficit (–) as a percentage of potential GNP*[a]

	1970	*1971*	*1972*	*1973*	*1974*	*1975*	*1976*	*1977*	*1978*	*1979*	*1980*	*1981*	*1982*	*1983*	*1984*	*1985*[b]
United States	0.0	–0.5	0.0	–0.2	–0.7	–0.9	0.4	0.6	0.9	1.2	0.7	1.0	0.1	–0.6	–1.4	–1.7
Japan	1.8	1.6	0.1	0.3	0.8	–1.9	–2.9	–3.1	–4.9	–4.2	–3.8	–3.4	–3.0	–2.4	–1.9	–1.1
Germany	–0.1	–0.2	0.0	1.3	–0.3	–3.2	–2.0	–1.0	–1.4	–2.0	–2.3	–2.6	–1.4	–0.1	0.4	1.0
France	0.9	0.7	0.4	0.4	0.7	–0.4	0.2	–0.2	–1.7	–0.9	0.4	–0.6	–1.1	–0.9	0.2	0.3
United Kingdom	2.3	0.9	–2.2	–4.9	–4.1	–4.0	–4.4	–2.8	–4.9	–4.0	–3.1	–0.2	1.3	0.0	–0.4	–0.2
Italy	–5.2	–6.7	–8.4	–8.3	–8.1	–10.1	–8.4	–7.3	–9.1	–9.7	–8.8	–12.5	–11.9	–10.2	–10.5	–10.4
Canada	1.3	0.1	–0.1	0.2	1.1	–2.4	–2.2	–2.2	–2.9	–1.6	–2.1	–1.3	–1.7	–3.4	–4.3	–5.3
Total for major seven countries[c]	0.3	–0.2	–0.6	–0.7	–0.2	–2.0	–1.4	–1.1	–1.7	–1.3	–1.3	–1.1	–1.3	–1.5	–1.7	–1.7
Australia	2.9	1.9	1.9	–1.1	2.0	–0.1	–2.6	1.0	–0.3	–0.8	–0.1	0.5	1.4	–1.3	–2.5	–3.1
Austria	1.6	2.6	2.2	2.0	2.7	–0.4	–2.2	–1.7	–0.7	–1.7	–1.2	–0.3	–1.0	–1.7	–0.6	–0.9
Belgium	–2.0	–2.3	–4.0	–4.8	–4.4	–3.9	–5.9	–4.1	–4.3	–4.6	–7.6	–11.1	–9.3	–8.8	–6.6	–5.4
Denmark	3.2	4.4	3.2	3.9	3.8	1.6	0.1	–0.1	0.7	–1.4	–1.1	–2.4	–5.6	–3.9	–2.3	–0.8
Finland	5.6	6.6	4.8	5.7	4.6	3.4	6.6	5.9	4.2	1.2	0.1	1.3	–0.6	–1.8	–0.1	–0.2

Greece	1.5	0.6	0.4	−1.4	0.0	−1.4	−0.8	0.1	0.0	−0.8	−0.9	−8.7	−3.5	−4.9	−6.0	−6.9
Netherlands	−0.8	−0.5	−0.4	−0.1	−1.1	−0.9	−1.9	−0.4	−0.8	−1.3	−1.6	−2.1	−2.2	−1.7	−2.0	−1.5
Norway	3.2	4.5	4.8	6.4	5.2	4.7	3.3	2.5	1.8	3.4	5.0	4.7	5.2	3.7	5.4	3.9
Spain	0.7	−0.3	0.1	0.4	−0.6	0.0	−0.3	−0.8	−1.7	−1.2	−1.2	−1.5	−3.3	−3.2	−2.8	−2.3
Sweden	4.4	5.9	5.2	4.0	0.8	1.6	3.9	3.7	2.2	−2.2	−2.8	−2.5	−2.8	−2.3	−1.5	−1.0
Total for smaller countries[c]	1.6	1.6	1.3	0.8	0.6	0.0	−0.6	0.2	−0.5	−1.3	−1.6	−2.1	−2.3	−2.6	−2.2	−2.1
Total for above countries[c]	0.5	0.0	−0.3	−0.5	−0.1	−1.8	−1.3	−0.9	−1.5	−1.3	−1.3	−1.2	−1.4	−1.6	−1.8	−1.7
Total excluding the United States	0.8	0.4	−0.6	−0.7	−0.7	−2.4	−2.4	−2.0	−3.2	−3.1	−2.8	−2.9	−2.5	−2.4	−2.0	−1.8

a. For the methodology used, see Price & Muller (1984). It must be noted that the figures shown in this table, as well as the changes in the cyclical and structural components of the deficit indicated in Table 1.3, have recently been revised by the OECD secretariat. This is due both to revisions in actual budget numbers and to changes in the method of calculation.
b. OECD estimates.
c. 1982 GNP weight and exchange rates.

SOURCE: OECD.

TABLE 1.5 *General government debt as a percentage of nominal GNP*

	Stock of Debt[a]						Debt Interest Payments					
	1970	*1975*	*1980*	*1983*	*1984*	*1985*[b]	*1970*	*1975*	*1980*	*1983*	*1984*	*1985*[b]
United States	46.2	44.7	39.5	45.0	45.8	48.3	1.2	1.2	1.3	2.1	2.4	2.6
Japan	12.0	22.5	52.9	68.2	69.3	69.4	0.6	1.2	3.2	4.4	4.6	4.8
Germany	18.4	24.9	32.5	41.1	41.9	42.2	1.0	1.4	1.9	3.0	3.0	3.0
France	29.4	25.8	25.0	29.8	31.8	34.0	1.1	1.3	1.6	2.6	2.8	2.8
United Kingdom	86.2	65.0	54.9	53.9	55.9	56.5	3.9	4.0	4.7	4.7	4.9	5.0
Italy	44.4	66.8	67.2	84.2	91.4	99.4	1.7	4.0	6.3	9.0	9.6	9.6
Canada	53.7	44.7	47.9	58.7	63.4	69.2	3.8	4.0	5.6	7.2	7.9	8.3
Total for seven major countries[c]	39.6	40.2	42.9	50.5	52.1	54.2	1.4	1.7	2.4	3.4	3.7	3.8
Australia	41.7	28.5	26.2	24.8	24.9	25.2	2.5	2.1	2.2	2.6	2.9	3.3
Austria	19.4	23.9	37.1	45.8	47.1	48.5	1.0	1.3	2.5	3.0	3.3	3.4
Belgium	73.3	65.8	82.8	115.6	121.8	126.6	3.4	3.5	6.0	9.4	10.1	10.3
Denmark	11.3	11.9	33.5	62.7	67.6	68.6	1.4	1.2	3.9	8.1	9.6	9.9

Finland	15.5	8.6	13.9	19.8	20.2	20.2	1.0	0.7	1.0	1.5	1.7	1.7
Greece	21.3	22.4	27.7	41.4	47.5	53.2	1.0	1.4	2.4	3.4	4.3	5.5
Ireland	66.8	72.3	87.7	113.2	119.1	128.3	3.7	4.2	6.5	10.0	10.4	11.8
Netherlands	51.4	41.3	45.9	62.3	66.9	70.3	2.9	3.9	3.7	5.7	6.1	6.4
Norway	48.4	48.2	55.9	42.6	36.1	31.4	1.8	2.1	3.9	3.8	3.9	5.2
Spain	14.4	13.0	17.6	31.8	38.4	41.7	0.6	0.5	0.8	1.3	1.8	2.2
Sweden	30.7	29.6	44.8	66.0	69.4	71.4	1.9	2.2	4.2	7.3	7.7	8.2
Total for small countries[c]	34.8	30.0	37.6	50.5	53.7	55.8	1.9	2.0	2.9	4.4	4.9	5.3
Total for above countries[c]	39.0	38.9	42.1	50.5	52.3	54.4	1.5	1.7	2.5	3.5	3.8	4.0

a. Gross debt outstanding at the end of each year.
b. OECD estimates.
c. 1982 GNP weights and exchange rates.

SOURCE: OECD.

TABLE 1.6 *Actual budget balances net of debt interest payments*[a], *as a percentage of nominal GNP*

	1970	1971	1972	1973	1974	1975	1976	1977	1978	1979	1980	1981	1982	1983	1984	1985[b]
United States	0.2	–0.7	0.7	1.7	0.8	–3.0	–0.8	0.3	1.3	1.8	0.1	0.8	–1.7	–2.0	–0.9	–1.2
Japan	2.4	1.9	0.7	1.5	1.4	–1.5	–2.1	–1.9	–3.3	–2.1	–1.3	–0.4	0.4	0.9	2.0	3.1
Germany	1.2	0.8	0.5	2.3	–0.1	–4.3	–1.9	–0.7	–0.8	–0.8	–1.0	–1.4	–0.5	0.5	1.1	1.8
France	2.1	1.8	1.7	1.8	1.6	–1.0	0.8	0.5	–0.4	0.9	1.8	0.3	–0.6	–0.5	0.0	–0.6
United Kingdom	6.4	5.0	1.7	0.3	0.5	–0.7	–0.6	1.0	0.1	1.1	1.2	2.2	2.7	1.0	1.0	1.6
Italy	–3.2	–5.1	–7.0	–6.1	–5.3	–7.7	–4.5	–3.0	–3.9	–3.7	–1.8	–4.7	–4.1	–3.4	–3.9	–3.9
Canada	4.7	4.0	4.0	4.9	5.6	1.5	2.5	2.0	1.8	3.5	2.9	4.8	2.3	1.0	1.5	1.8
Total for major seven countries[c]	1.3	0.5	0.6	1.3	0.7	–2.6	–1.0	–0.2	–0.2	0.5	0.0	0.3	–0.8	–0.8	–0.1	0.1
Australia	5.4	4.8	4.6	2.0	4.6	1.5	–0.8	1.9	0.7	0.0	0.9	1.9	2.3	–1.2	–0.3	0.4
Austria	2.1	2.5	3.0	2.3	2.3	–1.2	–2.1	–0.5	–0.5	–0.1	0.8	1.0	–0.1	–0.8	0.9	1.3
Belgium	1.4	0.3	–0.7	–0.2	0.9	–1.2	–1.7	–1.4	–1.5	–1.4	–2.4	–6.3	–3.3	–3.9	–1.2	0.2
Denmark	4.6	5.3	5.2	6.5	4.4	–0.1	1.1	1.3	1.9	1.8	0.7	–1.6	–3.1	0.8	5.3	7.5

Finland	5.3	5.4	4.7	6.5	5.2	3.3	5.5	3.9	2.2	1.4	1.6	2.4	0.9	–0.1	1.9	2.4
Greece	0.9	0.1	0.6	–0.4	–0.9	–2.1	–1.0	–1.7	–1.3	–0.2	–0.3	–8.7	–4.7	–6.0	–6.0	–6.0
Netherlands	2.2	2.5	2.9	4.1	3.4	0.8	0.8	1.5	0.9	–0.5	–0.5	–1.2	–2.1	–0.9	–0.4	1.1
Norway	5.0	6.1	6.5	7.7	6.7	5.9	5.6	4.5	3.9	7.1	9.9	8.6	8.2	7.6	10.1	10.5
Spain	1.3	0.0	0.8	1.7	0.7	0.5	0.1	–0.1	–1.2	–1.2	–1.2	–2.3	–4.4	–4.0	–3.2	–2.6
Sweden	6.3	7.2	6.3	6.0	4.0	4.9	6.6	4.2	2.2	0.2	0.4	0.5	0.9	2.2	4.4	5.8
Total for smaller countries[c]	3.3	3.1	3.1	3.2	2.9	1.1	1.0	1.3	0.4	0.1	0.3	–0.6	–0.9	–1.1	0.4	1.3
Total for above countries[c]	1.5	0.8	0.9	1.6	1.0	–2.1	–0.8	0.0	–0.1	0.5	0.1	0.2	–0.8	–0.9	0.0	0.2

a. General government financial surplus or deficit (–), as indicated in Table 1.1, less interest payments on public debt.
b. OECD estimates.
c. 1982 GNP weights and exchange rates.

SOURCE: OECD.

TABLE 1.7 *Ratio of budget deficit to gross private savings*[a]

	1970	1971	1972	1973	1974	1975	1976	1977	1978	1979	1980	1981	1982	1983	1984	1985[b]
United States	6.6	10.8	1.7	–3.4	2.0	22.9	12.3	5.5	–1.1	–3.6	7.1	5.3	22.0	23.1	18.2	22.5
Japan	–5.3	–3.9	0.3	–1.7	–1.3	9.5	12.1	13.1	18.2	16.6	15.6	14.2	13.2	12.9	9.6	6.1
Germany	–0.9	0.8	2.5	–6.0	6.4	27.2	17.0	12.9	12.5	12.6	14.6	18.7	16.6	12.2	9.4	5.6
France	–4.4	–3.5	–3.7	–4.4	–3.1	10.7	2.5	4.2	8.8	3.4	–1.1	9.8	15.3	17.3	15.5	18.3
United Kingdom	–17.2	–10.2	10.0	18.5	24.8	30.5	28.6	17.7	20.5	17.7	18.6	15.7	12.7	19.2	19.0	17.4
Italy	20.9	28.9	35.7	32.6	31.7	43.5	33.4	29.9	35.1	33.9	31.0	46.1	49.0	53.1	56.3	55.5
Canada	–5.5	–0.8	–0.4	–5.3	–9.8	12.5	8.5	12.6	15.5	8.1	11.9	7.4	24.1	28.1	28.1	28.6
Total for major seven countries[c]	1.8	5.5	3.9	0.2	4.1	20.9	14.0	10.7	11.1	8.9	12.3	12.8	20.3	21.1	18.0	18.8
Australia	–14.1	–11.4	–8.9	0.7	–10.4	2.6	14.1	3.5	10.0	10.7	6.6	1.2	0.2	22.3	17.9	16.9
Austria	–4.5	–6.7	–9.3	–6.0	–5.9	11.8	17.0	11.7	12.7	10.9	8.0	8.9	14.9	19.1	11.7	11.1
Belgium	8.2	13.0	16.7	15.0	11.1	21.6	23.5	25.5	27.2	30.7	39.2	66.4	60.5	58.0	50.9	44.3
Denmark	–14.9	–30.1	–24.9	–35.1	–22.2	8.4	1.7	3.8	2.3	12.1	23.2	45.5	51.3	44.3	28.7	16.6
Finland	–21.7	–23.1	–20.2	–30.4	–20.9	–13.8	–31.2	–18.9	–7.5	–2.1	–2.5	–6.7	2.0	7.3	–1.2	–3.2

Greece	0.3	3.4	1.0	4.3	8.1	14.7	10.5	8.4	6.3	8.3	9.5	47.0	39.7	45.3	46.2	52.0
Netherlands	2.9	1.8	2.3	−2.0	1.6	13.1	12.4	10.6	15.7	19.1	22.5	28.1	32.2	30.5	27.2	21.8
Norway	−15.8	−23.1	−25.7	−32.1	−23.8	−21.2	−18.1	−10.6	−3.6	−17.9	−29.5	−22.9	−22.4	−18.1	−29.7	−24.5
Spain	−3.3	2.6	−1.2	−5.4	−0.9	−0.2	1.6	3.5	8.8	9.2	11.3	17.3	29.3	30.4	25.9	24.5
Sweden	−31.6	−40.5	−33.4	−27.0	−12.0	−16.3	−35.7	−14.8	3.7	19.5	22.5	31.3	39.5	15.9	10.2	7.7
Total for smaller countries[c]	−6.8	−6.2	−5.3	−5.6	−3.9	4.5	5.4	6.2	11.3	13.6	15.0	22.4	25.7	26.6	20.3	18.1
Total for above countries[c]	0.8	4.1	2.7	−0.6	2.8	18.5	12.8	10.1	11.2	9.6	12.7	14.1	21.0	21.8	18.3	18.6

a. General government financial deficit as percentage of gross private savings. A negative sign indicates a financial surplus. Gross private savings = household + business gross savings, net of stock appreciation where data are available (for the United States, the United Kingdom and Canada) but before allowance for capital consumption.
b. OECD estimates.
c. Deficit and savings aggregated separately at current exchange rates.

SOURCE: OECD.

Increase in the Cost of Government Debt Service

As can be seen from Table 1.5, the general government debt service cost has risen quite considerably, partly because of increased public sector borrowing and partly because of higher interest rates due to the implementation of restrictive monetary policies. Thus, for the OECD area as a whole, debt interest payments, which represented 1.5 per cent of GDP in 1970, rose to 2.5 per cent in 1980 and reached 4 per cent in 1985. Over the same period, interest payments as a proportion of total government spending increased from 5.5 to 9.6 per cent. All OECD Member countries experienced a growth in the cost of servicing their public debt, and in many of them the ratio of this cost to GDP more than doubled between 1970 and 1985 (almost reaching or exceeding 10 per cent in Italy, Belgium and Ireland). Interest payments also increased rapidly in some countries, reflecting both intensive use of external financing and the rise in interest rates on international capital markets.

Excluding debt interest payments, the overall financial position of the general government sector in the seven largest OECD countries would, on average, have been more or less in equilibrium between 1970 and 1985 (see Table 1.6). This gives an insight to the seriousness of the problem of servicing government debt, particularly in countries such as the United States, Japan and Germany, where real interest rates on public sector borrowing have been strongly positive.[6] The fact is that continuous government borrowing to meet interest payment commitments on previous loans may well lead to an indefinite growth of the burden of public sector debt as a proportion of GDP. This risk is all the greater if interest rates, which are themselves pushed upwards by the accumulation of government borrowing, rise faster than GDP. In that case, interest payments to service existing debts would, in the long run, be equal to the budget deficit itself.[7] This explains why governments are at present taking steps to forestall such an eventuality by gradually reducing their deficits (see below).

The Impact of Inflation

The fact that public expenditure usually adjusts more quickly to inflation than tax receipts,[8] and that it may even rise faster than prices, is often considered to be one of the causes of the persistence of budget deficits. There are several reasons for this. On the one hand, the practice of automatic indexation of public sector pension and social security payments is widespread, which suggests that government expenditure in the form of transfers will rise in line with inflation. Some transfer payments are even 'over indexed'. This is true of those which are tied to a price index that tends to rise rapidly, either because it includes energy costs and indirect taxes or because the mechanisms for adjusting the index introduce a bias in an upward direction.[9] Moreover, to the extent that public sector wages and salaries tend to follow those paid in the private sector, the relative prices of public services tend to increase (productivity improvements being generally smaller in the public sector), which may result in higher government expenditure if corresponding forecasts do not take adequate account of this factor. Finally, wage and salary increases in the public sector sometimes exceed the forecasts, particularly during the 'catching-up' stage, when they are brought into line with the private sector, and this may also result in an excessive growth of government spending.

The effect of inflation on government debt service payments may be analysed as follows:

- When inflation expectations rise (meaning that financial markets expect price increases to accelerate in the future) long-term interest rates tend to be higher, which increases the government debt service cost, and, in turn, the budget deficit.
- When inflation speeds up suddenly and unexpectedly, interest payments on the *existing* government debt fall in real terms (since the yields of bonds issued in the past prove to be lower than the current inflation rate). In other words, holders of government securities suffer capital losses – as a result of the depreciation of their financial assets – while total government spending tends to fall.
- When deflationary policies are accompanied by a rise in real interest rates, the burden of debt servicing on the government may be further increased.

The link between inflation and government debt interest payments raises a particular problem as regards the interpretation of the stance of fiscal policy.[10] For example, if the capital gains resulting from the depreciation of government debt due to inflation had been added to government revenue, the financial position of the general government sector in the seven major OECD countries would have been broadly in balance in 1980 and 1981 (when prices were rising rapidly) whereas it was actually in deficit. From this point of view, fiscal policy may be considered to have been more restrictive than intended: this is illustrated by Table 1.3 (line 4), which shows the changes in structural budget balances, adjusted for the effects of inflation on government debt. Conversely, the decline in the rate of inflation during 1983–84 had the effect of reducing the 'inflation tax' on the holders of government bonds, and since, at the same time, nominal interest rates remained relatively high the burden of government debt increased in real terms. The inflation-adjusted balance of OECD governments therefore tended to worsen,[11] with the result that fiscal policy proved to be less restrictive than expected. Though adjustment to allow for the effects of price increases is useful from an analytical point of view, it should not be concluded that governments should formulate their fiscal policy to take account of inflation, by targeting explicitly a budget balance objective expressed in real terms.

Discretionary Action to Support Output and Employment

Compared with the combined effects of the slowdown in economic activity, the rise in the cost of government debt service and the acceleration of inflation, the measures adopted by governments in order to stimulate activity have played a relatively less important role in the increase in budget deficits since the beginning of the 1970s. As noted above, the changes in the cyclically adjusted (or structural) budget balances set out in Table 1.3 (line 3) give some idea of the discretionary fiscal actions of OECD governments during the period 1970–85. As can be seen from the table, the stimulative budget measures adopted throughout this period accounted for almost 2 per cent of GDP. Three distinct phases of expansiory budget action can be identified.[12]

- The first phase, covering the years 1971–72, occurred in a context of generalised monetary expansion, in conjunction with the transition to a system of floating exchange rates;
- The second phase corresponds to the collective reaction of the OECD governments to the recession caused by the oil shock of 1973–74; it was characterised by a serious deterioration of the overall OECD budget balance of around 3.5 per cent of GDP in 1975 (see Table 1.1). This was a reflection of governments' desire

to accept the external deficits due to the oil shock and to counteract their negative effects on economic activity by allowing increases in budget deficits;

- The third phase of budgetary expansion occurred during 1978–79, after the adoption of coordinated pressures by the largest OECD countries, in which Germany and Japan have been the most active.

Since 1980, on the other hand, the dominant tendency has been towards budgetary restrictions as governments have been attempting to reduce their budget deficits, mainly by cutting back their expenditure. However, two major exceptions should be noted in this respect:

- In France an expansionary fiscal policy was implemented in the spring of 1981 through increased public spending (particularly in the form of transfer payments) with a view to sustaining economic activity and reducing unemployment. Given the difficulties arising from the subsequent deterioration of the balance of payments, the fall in the external value of the franc and the persistence of inflationary pressures, the direction of fiscal policy was reversed in the autumn of 1982 and again further in the spring of 1983 (the budget deficit being limited to 3 per cent of GDP).
- In the United States, the policy implemented in 1981 resulted in a sizeable increase in the federal budget deficit, due to a gradual reduction in income taxes and a rise in defence spending. Although this policy was based on the assumption that the tax cuts would be offset by a simultaneous reduction in non-defence government spending, the pressure put on Congress in order to achieve these spending cuts proved only partly successful.

1.2 THE EFFECTS OF PUBLIC SECTOR DEFICITS ON ECONOMIC ACTIVITY

Against the background of slowed economic growth and increased unemployment, some doubts have been expressed regarding the efficacy of fiscal policies as a means of supporting economic activity and employment. Certain mechanisms may in fact weaken the expansionary impact of budget deficits: the output gains resulting from such deficits may be partly or totally offset by the 'crowding-out' effects of private demand. This section analyses the nature of these effects and discusses the medium-term consequences of public sector deficits. To start with, it should be emphasised that since the mid-1970s fiscal policy has usually been implemented within a framework of explicit targets for monetary growth (or credit expansion) and floating exchange rates. It is important to bear this in mind when analysing the effects of public deficits on economic activity.

Real 'Crowding-Out' Effects

In general, the implementation of a public sector deficit is based on the desirability of compensating for 'excess' private sector savings (i.e. the net financial surplus of households and companies). However, an increase in the government's borrowing requirement may, in practice, be accompanied by an offsetting rise in private savings; it may also result in a deterioration in the external trade balance because of an increase in imports. These consequences which are often referred to as 'real crowding out', tend to limit the expansionary impact of fiscal policy on output. They may happen whether or not the monetary authorities decide to accommodate the budget deficit.

Imports' leakages

When the economy is extremely dependent on imports, part of the stimulatory effect of an expansionary fiscal policy will be lost because of the deterioration in the current account of the balance of payments. This is most likely when the authorities tend to stabilise the exchange rate and interest rates, which means that they are operating in a fixed exchange rate system and are implementing an accommodating monetary policy. Such a strategy involves a high risk of failure, since the resulting fall in foreign exchange reserves and the downward pressure on the exchange rate may compel the authorities to reverse the stance of their fiscal and monetary policies through the adoption of higher taxes and increases in interest rates. If that happens, the initial expansionary effect via the budget will be neutralised. The experience of France between 1981 and 1983 provides a good illustration of this kind of situation.

Allowing the exchange rate to float does not necessarily increase the authorities' room for manoeuvre. In that case, as the examples of the United Kingdom and Italy during the second half of the 1970s demonstrate, the combination of an expansiory fiscal stance with a policy of monetary accommodation may result in a vicious circle of inflation and falling exchange rates. As a result, the economic instability and the climate of uncertainty will make inevitable the adoption of austerity measures along with restrictions on the growth of the money supply.

Possible reactions of private savings

The private sector's saving behaviour may also neutralise the expansionary effects of a budget deficit. If the deficit is financed through money creation, the resulting acceleration of inflation may induce households to increase their savings in order to preserve the real value of their financial assets. The counterpart to this will be a fall in private demand, thus cancelling out the effects of the fiscal stimulus. The saving behaviour of households observed during the 1970s tended to corroborate the views of those who argued that some degree of crowding-out of demand did in fact take place in this way.[13]

Even in cases where the budget deficit is financed through non-inflationary channels, i.e. by resorting to non-bank borrowing, it may be accompanied by a compensatory increase in private sector savings. This is the case particularly when households assimilate public expenditure to their own consumption: private demand is then likely to be directly crowded out. Similarly, if households expect that taxes will be raised in the future in order to reimburse the public sector debt, they may well be led to make appropriate provisions accordingly.

All depends, however, on the way in which the government spends the money it borrows. If the proceeds of government borrowing are used to finance consumption, households may react by making an extra effort to save so as to be able to cope with future tax liabilities; this militates against the use of public consumption as an instrument of expansionary fiscal policy.[14] If, on the other hand, government borrowing is intended to finance profitable public investment or is used to stimulate private investment, the budget deficit may be seen as a contribution to economic growth. In this latter case, households will be less inclined to increase their savings, which will limit the risk of a reduction in private demand.

Financial 'Crowding-Out' Effects

While the effectiveness of a budget stimulus in supporting economic activity may be reduced by offsetting increases in private savings, or import leakages, the main doubts about the impact of fiscal policy on output have centred on the issue of 'financial crowding-out'. This usually means the negative effects that upward pressures on interest rates, coupled with an accumulation of public sector borrowing, may have on investment by the private sector. In this context, the main question is whether a bond-financed increase in the budget deficit – i.e. one that does not imply money creation – displaces a proportionate amount of private demand, thereby offsetting any net stimulatory effect of fiscal policy on national income. Such a crowding out of private spending may be avoided if additional sources of financing can be found, either through the money-bond substitution in private portfolios or the attraction of foreign capital. Moreover, the effects of government debt accumulation on the size and composition of net wealth may also influence private expenditure.

Transactions crowding-out

If a monetary target is adhered to, an increase in budget deficit financed by borrowing in capital markets will raise aggregate demand only if, through higher interest rates, money holders can be induced to substitute cash for government bonds while maintaining their spending. A given money stock could then finance a higher level of activity as the private sector economises on its cash balances, i.e. tends to hold less money in its asset portfolio. However, to the extent that private spending and borrowing are reduced by higher interest rates, some private demand will be displaced. The net result may be an overall expansion of domestic demand but changes in its composition as private borrowers are crowded out from capital markets. In the extreme case where cash balances are not reduced by higher interest rates while private spending is affected by the increased cost of credit, a bond-financed increase in the budget deficit would result only in the displacement of private borrowers, leaving aggregate demand and activity unaffected.

The importance of these effects depends on the interest elasticity of the demand for money and of private expenditure. The more interest elastic the demand for money and the less interest elastic are private consumption and investment, the less crowding out will be associated with bond-financed increases in the budget deficit. The evidence in this respect is generally not conclusive.[15] Stable interest rate elasticities of the demand for money and/or private expenditure items are difficult to identify. Moreover, in some countries, administrative rationing of credit implies that interest rates may frequently be poor measures of the cost of credit. It is worth noting that in such countries, somewhat paradoxically, 'crowding-out' effects are likely to be greater. This is because the private sector does not have the incentive to economise on holdings of money balances, which would otherwise have been stimulated by the rise in interest rates.

In an open economy, private borrowers displaced from the domestic credit markets may borrow from abroad, thus providing another channel through which private expenditure may be maintained in the face of a bond-financed fiscal stimulus. Indeed, if the exchange rate is fixed or managed, the money supply will rise (because of central bank interventions in the exchange market), in which case crowding out is not an issue. But if, in attempting to maintain its monetary target, the central bank avoids intervening in the exchange market, allowing the currency to float, the outcome will depend on the extent to which foreign capital supplements the domestic sources of finance. The more sensitive foreign capital is to interest rate differentials, the smaller would be both the domestic interest rate increase needed to fund the budget deficit and the potential crowding out of private spending. In this case, however, capital inflows may result in an appreciation of the exchange rate affecting exports and import competing industries. A fiscal stimulus, combined with non-accommodating monetary policy, may then lead to a form of 'exchange rate crowding out' where the budget deficit has its counterpart in a deficit of the current account of the balance of payments.

The extent to which the attraction of foreign capital may permit an effective and independent fiscal policy is thus limited. The transmission of interest rate pressures throughout the OECD area (as appears to have occurred as a result of the combination of high budget deficits and strict monetary control in the United States) may even lead to *international* financial crowding out of private demand, and to a situation where the high costs of government borrowing act as a deterrent against public sector deficits.

Portfolio crowding-out

Even where the private sector reduces its money holdings in response to higher interest rates, thus allowing the budget deficit to be financed without money creation, continuous public sector borrowing may imply increasing imbalances between government bonds and other financial assets in private portfolios. The absorption of excess bonds by the private sector could then imply a cumulative upward pressure on interest rates. This 'portfolio crowding out' may be of particular significance when government bonds form a growing proportion of outstanding debt; in this case the demand impulse of the budget deficit would be progressively negated by reductions in interest-sensitive private expenditures.

However, if the fiscal stimulus is partially effective, private sector accumulation of financial assets may increase as a result of higher private savings (i.e. increased wealth). The enhanced supply of funds may then offset upward pressure on interest rates in capital markets, so that the crowding out of private borrowers would be limited. There might even be a 'crowding in' effect on private investment, with an increase in interest-sensitive private expenditure. This would be the case where bond issues to finance the budget deficit are sufficiently short-term and liquid as to be excellent substitutes for money.[16] The existence of close money substitutes might, however, be seen as evidence that the money aggregate monitored by the authorities is badly defined and could undermine the effectiveness of target-oriented monetary policy designed to control inflation.

The wealth increase generated by the fiscal impulse is, of course, uncertain. Empirical evidence on this issue is even less conclusive than on the interest rate elasticities of the demand for money and private expenditure discussed above. The financing of government deficits is less likely to cause problems if accompanied by high private saving rates. In such a case, the greater the increase in the demand for financial assets (if individual, have a marginal preference for holding securities rather than money) the greater the possibility of a fall in capital market interest rates. Budgetary expansion might then be self sustaining because of its beneficial effects on both asset accumulation and capital formation.

But even with a relatively large degree of substitutability between government debt and money, it is not clear whether the asset accumulation by the private sector will necessarily prove beneficial. Money balances may, in fact, be positively related to wealth, so that crowding out may be exacerbated because a greater increase in interest rates would be necessary to choke off the additional demand for money. Nevertheless, the asset accumulation argument has provided an important rationale for a demand supportive long-run budget stance (in the form of steady government debt accumulation) in those countries (notably Germany, Japan, the Netherlands and Austria) where household savings ratios are usually high.

The Medium-Term Consequences of Public Sector Deficits

The above analysis leads to the conclusion that, to the extent that private sector savings increase and are used to purchase additional governments bonds, a certain level of budget deficit is not necessarily incompatible with the achievement of a specific monetary target. Therefore, a balanced budget rule is in no sense the best strategy to pursue. An accumulation of public sector deficits may, however, have undesirable consequences in the medium term because of its effects of interest rates, inflationary expectations and the cost of servicing government debt. These are precisely the concerns underlying the policies of budget restriction which are currently being implemented in a large number of countries.

Continued increases in public sector borrowing, in the absence of an accommodating monetary policy, may lead to an imbalance between the overall supply of and demand for credit. Such an imbalance will provoke upward pressure on long-term interest rates, and if, as a result, the corporate sector is led to resort more to short-term loans, the whole structure of interest rates will be affected. Conversely, the persistence of budget deficits may give rise to fears of 'monetisation' of public debt (monetary policy being relaxed in order to facilitate both the financing of increased government borrowing and the existing private demand for credit). This may strengthen inflationary expectations if, as a consequence, economic agents anticipate an acceleration in the rate of price increase. In order to protect themselves against such an eventuality, savers will then tend to claim for higher real interest rates.

Whatever the situation, therefore, the prospect of high budget deficits is likely to result in a rise in interest rates, which may be damaging in the medium term for both investment and output. The changes in the ratio of government borrowing requirements to private savings (see Table 1.7) do not, of course, necessarily confirm the existence of a direct link between budget deficits and interest rates. They do, however, tend to support the idea of a relationship between *expected* deficits and rises in long-term rates. In other words, future budget deficits may well influence current interest rates.

Moreover, as indicated above, accumulating public sector deficits imply an increase in the cost of government debt servicing which, when real interest rates are positive, may appear unsustainable in the long run. The risk is then that the situation may deteriorate to the point that it becomes necessary, in order to meet the debt interest payments, to cut other categories of public spending (or even raise taxes) so as to avoid having to resort to money creation. In such a case, the expansionary effect of a budget deficit on demand would gradually tend to diminish. In short, therefore, once public sector deficits become structural, the role of fiscal policy as an instrument to support activity and employment becomes more and more limited.

1.3 THE LINK BETWEEN PUBLIC SECTOR DEFICITS, MONETARY GROWTH AND INFLATION

The fixation of limits to monetary growth, and the attempts made by governments to finance budget deficits through bond issues, may partly be justified by the notion that the link between budget deficits and inflation (or inflationary expectations) relies on money creation. From this point of view, inflation is seen as being mainly a monetary phenomenon; in other words, expansion of the money supply is considered to be a factor which, in the medium term, determines the rate of price increases.

In accounting terms, bank loans to the public sector constitute one of the counterparts to the money supply. There is, therefore, a direct link between government borrowing requirements and money creation, to the extent that such borrowings are financed by the central bank and the commercial banks (in the form of loans to the Treasury or the purchase of government securities). The authorities may, however, attempt to limit the monetary financing of the budget deficit by selling government securities to the non-bank private sector (households, companies, and financial institutions other than banks). In that case, there is no effect on the money supply, as assets are transferred from the private sector to the government and vice versa when the money is spent by the authorities.

Whatever the method of financing considered,[17] the effect of the budget deficit on monetary growth will depend mainly on the attitude of the monetary authorities (i.e. whether they decide to accommodate the deficit increase, by allowing the money supply to expand, or not). In practice, the authorities take into account anticipated variations in budget deficits when implementing their policy. But different implications for the money supply, consequent upon a given change in the budget deficit, may arise depending on institutional arrangements for monetary control. Although these differ among countries, they may broadly be divided into two groups:[18] Type I and Type II systems.

In Type I systems, the authorities mainly operate on the *portfolio behaviour of the banking sector* in order to control monetary growth. To this end, the central bank provokes changes in banks' cash reserves, in particular through its money market operations and its loans to the banks, as part of its refinancing policy. Interest rates adjust to equate demand and supply in money and credit markets, and there is no resort to administrative controls on bank credit. A basic characteristic of such systems is, moreover, that the 'monetisation' of public debt is in no sense automatic. In the absence of any accommodation by the central bank, an increase in the budget deficit will initially result in a rise in interest rates (since the demand for credit from the public sector will increase while the banks' ability to supply credit will remain unchanged). In other words, the growth of the money supply will not be affected by the increase in government borrowing.

Type II systems are characterised, on the other hand, by attempts to control the money supply through its asset counterparts. For this purpose the authorities seek to influence mainly the *behaviour of the non-bank private sector* via administered interest rates. Typically, interest rates are set to influence the private sector's demand for bank credit and government bonds. For a given budget deficit, the volume of government borrowing from the banks will then be dependent on the demand for credit from the private sector. At given interest rates, the banking system is supposed to cover the share of the budget deficit that is not financed by private savings. Consequently, in Type II systems, unexpected increases in the budget deficit, against a background of unchanged interest rates, will tend to provoke an expansion of bank credit and thus of the money supply. The banks in fact will generally tend to satisfy the increased government borrowing needs as well as the private sector demand for credit, unless the central bank raises its interest rates and/or establishes ceilings on bank credit expansion.

This suggests, therefore, that the financing of budget deficits is less problematic for the control of monetary growth when such control operates through action on bank liquidity (Type I systems) rather than through the counterparts of the money supply (Type II systems). In Type II systems the authorities do, of course, have the option of raising interest rates in order to neutralise the effect of an increase in the budget deficit on the growth of the money supply. In view, however, of the difficulty of forecasting fluctuations in the deficit, there may be some overshooting of the money supply growth targets in the short run. To the extent that the achievement of such targets is thought to be important in the context of inflation control, the efficacy of monetary policy is likely to be reduced.

Though Type I systems of monetary control do appear, therefore, to offer some advantages as regards the financing of public sector deficits, they are not necessarily as helpful with respect to the co-ordination of monetary and fiscal policies. Since in such systems the central bank is not automatically involved in the financing of the budget deficit, control of monetary growth may operate independently of the stance of fiscal policy. It follows from this that the authorities may, in principle, attempt simultaneously to control inflation by setting monetary targets and support economic activity by implementing bond financed budget deficits. As the recent experience in the United States suggests, however, independent use of monetary and fiscal policies may be hampered by the medium-term consequences arising from an accumulation of budget deficits. In particular, as noted above, such deficits may give rise to inflationary expectations if the capital markets expect a rapid expansion of the money supply in order to finance increased public sector borrowing.

1.4 THE MOVE TOWARDS THE REDUCTION OF PUBLIC SECTOR DEFICITS

A number of common features in the attitudes of governments with respect to fiscal policy emerge from the experience of the last five years:

- there is growing scepticism about the effectiveness of the independent use of fiscal policy to support economic activity (the example of France during 1981–82 is particularly significant in this respect);
- there is a general tendency towards the adoption of consistent policies in a medium-term context as a substitute for systematic interventions designed to regulate economic activity; this reflects the desire to create a climate of stability which will be favourable to companies' decisions on investment and production;
- there is a need for better co-ordination of the use of monetary and fiscal instruments:[19] in fact, with the adoption of explicit targets for

money growth or credit expansion, fiscal policy has ceased to be an autonomous instrument and has tended to be subordinated to monetary policy. In other words, firm control of public sector borrowing has been seen as an indispensable prerequisite for the achievement of the monetary targets.

These considerations underly the move towards fiscal retrenchment in OECD countries. This section discusses the policies adopted to this end and the progress achieved so far.

Policies adopted

The policies implemented in the OECD countries with a view to cutting budget deficits have mostly been guided by the same objective: the reduction of the size of the public sector by curbing the growth of current expenditure and by allowing a decline of the tax burden. However, different approaches have been followed in the major countries in order to achieve this objective, which may be broadly classified as follows:

- those as 'budget consolidation processes' qualified, aimed at gradually restoring budget balance by a reduction of government expenditure (e.g. in Germany and in the United Kingdom) and, where necessary, raising taxes (as in Japan);
- those known as 'supply-side' strategies, based on a simultaneous cut in taxes and public spending (this was the case in particular in the United States during the year 1981–84).

With the first approach, the cuts in public spending were designed to reduce public sector borrowing and interest rates in the first instance and then taxes. In other words, the decline in the tax burden was regarded as the final step in the process of budget consolidation. Consequently, reducing the budget deficit was generally considered to be more important than tax cuts for promoting economic recovery.

With the second approach, on the other hand, cutting taxes was given priority over budget deficit reductions. In the United States, for example, pending the adoption by Congress of measures designed to reduce government spending, it was recognised that tax cuts would be reflected in an increase in the budget deficit. This was considered to involve the risk of an increased preemption of available savings by the Government and, therefore, a rise in interest rates. While admitting that the budget deficit may crowd out private investors from financial markets and create unfavourable consequences for future economic growth, 'supply-siders' point out that government borrowing is equivalent to tax financing with respect to the impact on interest rates. There are two reasons for this:[20]

- Tax-payers may save in anticipation of the taxes they will have to pay in the future; in that case interest rates are hardly affected since the increase in government borrowing leads to a proportional rise in private savings.
- Moreover, to the extent that tax cuts are mainly beneficial to the corporate sector, companies will have additional resources to finance their investments. As a result, their demand for credit will fall, thus making room for an increase in public sector borrowing on capital markets.

In many countries the authorities have attempted to restructure the tax system and public spending in favour of enterprises. In this respect the arguments of the proponents of supply-side policies do not apply only to the United States. On the other hand, the principle of a reduction in taxes accompanied by a rise in the budget deficit is not so universally accepted, although it is based on the conviction that tax cuts that result in a redistribution of income in favour of the corporate sector may be beneficial for investment and growth. The prevailing opinion, in fact, is that, on the one hand, public sector deficits contribute to upward pressure on interest rates and, on the other, the persistent federal deficit in the United States, by transmitting high real interest rates to Europe and Japan and heavily affecting the international indebtedness of the developing countries, may well be a source of international crowding out of private demand.

Progress achieved

The budget balances set out in Table 1.1 give some idea of the progress achieved in recent years as regards the reduction of public sector deficits. Throughout the OECD area as a whole, the *actual* deficit of the general government sector, which reached a maximum of 4.5 per cent of GDP in 1983, fell for the first time in 1984 (to a level of 3.9 per cent of GDP). This trend continued during 1985. Among the largest Member countries, considerable progress was achieved in Germany, Japan and in the United Kingdom: in these three countries the deficit came down in 1985 to a level lower than that in 1979. In the United States and France, on the other hand, the general government financial position tended to deteriorate, while in Canada and Italy (countries with deficits still representing a large proportion of GDP) it has remained a serious source of concern. As for the smaller economies, reduction in the budget deficit was recorded in most of them, but in some cases (notably Belgium, Ireland and Greece) the deficit remains particularly high.

The more restrictive stance of fiscal policy in recent years has been reflected in a reduction of the general government *structural* deficit in the OECD area as a whole, excluding the United States: as a proportion of GDP, the deficit has fallen from 3 per cent in 1979 to 1.8 per cent in 1985 (see Table 1.4). This trend has been particularly marked in Germany (which has registered a structural surplus since 1983) and, to a smaller extent, in Japan. In the United States, in contrast, the structural budget balance has deteriorated from +1.2 per cent of GDP in 1979 to −1.7 per cent in 1985. Judging by present projections, this situation is likely to continue in coming years. The move towards a reduction in budget deficits in the OECD countries (excluding the United States) has not been accompanied by a diminution in the share of public sector revenue and expenditure in GDP. In fact, as shown in Table 1.2b the tax burden in this group of countries increased by about 4 per cent between 1979 and 1985 (on a cyclically adjusted basis). On the spending side, the increase is smaller, of the order of 2.5 per cent, and is mainly a reflection of the increase in debt interest payments. Two large countries – Germany, and, to a lesser extent, the United Kingdom – constitute exceptions to this trend: in Germany public spending as a proportion of GDP has fallen by 3.5 per cent, while in the United Kingdom it has dropped by about 1 per cent.

The situation in the United States differs from that in the other OECD countries mainly as regards revenue, the share of which in GDP fell slightly between 1979 and 1985 (see Table 1.2a). Government expenditure, on the other hand, increased over the same period by almost 2.5 per cent of GDP, more than half being attributable to the cost of servicing public sector debt. This contrast between the respective trends of government revenue and spending provides a good illustration of the importance of the budgetary choices with which the US authorities are presently confronted.

NOTES

1. These issues have been analysed in detail in some recent OECD publications. See, in particular, Chouraqui & Price (1983, 1984), Price & Muller (1984) and OECD (1982).
2. The changes in the budget balances resulting from 'discretionary' actions by the authorities incorporate fiscal drag as well as any budgetary shortfalls and overruns. Therefore, they do represent a strict measure of the policymakers' intentions, although failure to adjust tax thresholds in line with inflation may be considered as a deliberate action on the part of the government. Conversely, measurements of the effects of the automatic stabilisers may vary because of alterations in unemployment benefit rates; this component does therefore contain an element of discretionary action. The calculation method used is described in Chouraqui & Price (1983), page 39. For a detailed discussion of the problems and issues involved in measuring cyclically adjusted budget deficits, see de Leeuw & Holloway (1982), Fellner (1983), and Price & Muller (1984).
3. A comparative analysis of structural budget deficits may be found in Price & Muller (1984) and in Chouraqui & Price (1984b).
4. Replacement ratios, the duration of employment benefits and the degree of supplementary income support may all affect the supply of labour. Empirical studies have usually concluded that unemployment insurance tends to cause the unemployment rate to rise because of the increased time spent in job research and greater incentives to join the registered labour force. Moreover, social security systems may increase wage and salary costs per person employed, to such an extent that it may constitute a disincentive to recruit permanent, full-time staff (a situation sometimes referred to as a 'welfare state crisis').
5. See, for example, OECD (1981) and Danziger (1981).
6. See in this respect Congressional Budget Office (1984).
7. The outstanding debt/GDP ratio would tend to a ceiling of $b[(1+g)/g]$, where b is the ratio of the budget deficit to GDP and g is the growth rate of GDP. In a continuous time formulation, this becomes b/g, from which it follows that if the interest rate was equivalent to the growth rate then the debt interest payments, as a proportion of GDP, would become equal to b.
8. Though, in principle, a system of progressive taxation automatically results in an increase in the tax burden because of the effect of inflation, in parallel with the rise in nominal incomes, developments observed since the beginning of the 1970s have tended to some extent to correct the effects of this phenomenon. This widespread adoption of systems of fiscal indexation has meant that the rise in tax revenue has not necessarily been proportional to inflation. This explains, among other things, why the elasticity of tax revenue with respect to inflation has fallen below one in several OECD countries.
9. This is true of certain categories of transfer payments in the United States; see *United States Congress* (1976).
10. See Price & Muller (1984).
11. See *OECD Economic Outlook* no. 35, July 1984.

12. For further details, see Chouraqui & Price (1984), pp. 10–20.
13. A negative effect on private consumption, linked to the erosion of the value of financial assets as a result of inflation, has been observed in the United States, Japan and the United Kingdom. It should be pointed out, however, that while inflation reduces the value of financial claims it also reduces the burden of debt. For this reason, account should be taken of the overall effects of the distribution of wealth between creditors and debtors. On this point, see Tobin (1980).
14. Research in this field, however, has not produced conclusive results. See, for example, Stevens (1979) and Feldstein (1982).
15. See OECD (1982), pp. 35–40.
16. On this point, see Freidman (1978).
17. A detailed analysis of the various methods of financing the budget deficit may be found in OECD (1982) and Chouraqui (1984).
18. In this respect, see OECD (1982). Apart from the United States, whose system of monetary control is typical of Type I (especially since the introduction, in November 1979, of a new procedure based on the regulation of bank reserves), the classification of the other major countries is, in practice, not so clear-cut. To some extent, the systems of monetary control adopted in Germany and Canada belong broadly to Type I. Those used in Japan, France, the United Kingdom and Italy, on the other hand, are closer to Type II. In this latter group of countries, however, a number of changes has been introduced recently in the conduct of monetary policy, notably the abolition of credit ceilings and the implementation of greater interest rate flexibility. This tends to make these countries moving towards Type I systems of monetary control.
19. This aspect has been examined in detail in Chouraqui & Price (1984).
20. Cf. United States Treasury (1984). This study contains several bibliographical references on the link between deficits and interest rates.

REFERENCES

Chouraqui, J-C. (1984) 'Budget Deficits, Monetary Growth and Financial Crowding-out' in 'Government Policies and the Working of Financial systems in Industrialized Countries', *Proc. SUERF Conf.* (The Netherlands. Martinus Nijhoff).

Chouraqui, J-C. & R. Price (1983) 'Public Sector Deficits: Problems and Policy Implications', *OECD Occasional Studies*, June.

Chouraqui, J-C. & R. Price (1984) 'Medium-Term Financial Strategy: The Co-ordination of Fiscal and Monetary Policies', *OECD Economic Studies*, no. 2.

Chouraqui, J-C. & R. Price (1986) 'Budget Deficits in Europe and the United States: Fiscal Policy Asymmetry and the Sustainability of the Current Recovery', in 'Europe and the Dollar', Banco San Paolo di Torino, June.

Congress of the United States (1976) 'The Effect of Inflation on Federal Expenditure, *Background Paper*, no. 9.

Congressional Budget Office (1984) 'Federal Debt and Interest Costs', *Congress of the United States*, Sep.

Danzinger *et al.* (1981) 'How Income Transfer Programs Affect Work, Savings and the Income Distribution: A Critical Review', *Journal of Economic Literature*, Sep.

de Leeuw, H. & J. M. Holloway (1982) 'The High Employment Budget: Revised Estimates and Automatic Inflation Effects', *Survey of Current Business*, US Department of Commerce, April.

Feldstein, M. (1982) 'Government Deficits and Aggregate Demand', *Journal of Monetary Economics*, no. 9.

Fellner, W. (1982) 'The High Employment Budget and Potential Output', *Survey of Current Business*, US Department of Commerce, Nov.

Friedman, B. M. (1978) 'Crowding Out or Crowding In? Economic Consequences of Financial Government Deficits', *Brookings Papers on Economic Activity*, no. 3.

OECD (1981) *The Welfare State in Crisis*.

OECD (1982) *Budget Financing and Monetary Control*, OECD Monetary Studies Series.

Price, R. & P. Muller (1984) 'Structural Budget Indicators and the Interpretation of Fiscal Policy Stance in OECD Economies', *OECD Economic Studies*, no. 3.

Tobin, J. (1980) 'Stabilization Policy Ten Years After', *Brookings Papers on Economic Activity*, no. 1.

Stevens, N. A. (1979) Government Debt Financing – its Effects in View of Tax Discounting', *Federal Reserve Bank of Saint Louis, Quarterly Review*, July.

United States Treasury (1984) 'The Effect of Deficits on Prices of Financial Assets: Theory and Evidence'.

2 The Consequences of Persistent Large Budget Deficits

Rudolph G. Penner

A sharp rise in federal deficits in the last few years and projections of a string of very large deficits beyond the end of this decade have been accompanied by a heated public debate about their consequences. The projections indicate that under policies currently in place, eight consecutive years of fairly brisk uninterrupted economic growth would leave the ratio of federal budget deficits relative to GNP, higher than any experienced in peacetime prior to 1982. Such deficits would add rapidly to the federal debt and would also greatly increase the share of GNP that must be devoted to servicing this debt.

Budget deficits, even of the size recently experienced and projected for the next several years, are unlikely to have a sudden destructive impact on the economy. Over a short period they may even have invigorating effects in many sectors, boosting employment and real after-tax incomes, although some sectors – primarily export- and import-competing industries – may not share in the general prosperity. Under some circumstances, the overall consequences of temporary deficits, even of large ones, could be beneficial rather than detrimental to the economy. If large deficits persist, however, as CBO projects they will unless the policy is substantially altered, their stimulative effect will wear off and adverse consequences will begin to appear. It may be a long time before these begin to be translated into stagnating or perhaps even declining standards of living, deteriorating public services, or reduced defense capabilities. But even though the damage may be initially difficult to detect, it would become progressively more difficult to undo as the erosion of productive capacity proceeded. This chapter discusses the adverse effects of persistently large deficits in some detail.

Persistently large deficits are opposed for a variety of reasons: that they lead to unusually high real interest rates; that they channel an increasing portion of available savings into federal use; and that they have destructive effects on the foreign-trade sector. Some believe that large deficits will eventually lead to increased inflation. But while some hints of these and other related consequences of large deficits can be found in economic history, there is no general agreement on the likelihood of those dangers, nor on their magnitude or timing.

One reason for the lack of consensus as to the precise effects of deficits is that the Keynesian theory, which dominated economics until the 1970s, is no longer generally accepted and has not been replaced by another dominant theory. A more important reason for the diversity of views is that experience with very large and persistent deficits during peacetime is quite limited. As a result, it is extremely difficult to obtain solid empirical confirmation or refutation of competing hypotheses formed on the basis of theoretical reasoning.

Despite the resulting diversity of views on the consequences of persistent large budget deficits, the vast majority of economists believe that the present outlook for US fiscal policy is fraught with dangers. One reason is that the deficits are so large in relation to historical experience. But there are also well-founded theoretical reasons for worrying about large deficits. The purpose of this chapter is to discuss some of their consequences in the short run and the long run.[1]

The discussion that follows assumes that any effort to reduce deficits would take the form of across-the-board spending cuts or tax increases. (This is not a forecast or a recommendation, but simply a convenient assumption made solely for analytical purposes.) The discussion assumes further that any negative effects the tax and spending changes might have on economic efficiency would be outweighed by the beneficial effects of deficit reduction. Not all would agree with this; some would place more emphasis on the possible negative consequences. It is indeed possible to think of spending cuts or tax changes that would have very negative effects. But in order to focus on the economic consequences of deficits *per se*, it is assumed that negative effects are kept at a minimum.

2.1 THE ADVERSE SHORT-TERM CONSEQUENCES OF LARGE DEFICITS

The short term approximates a world in which stocks of assets and liabilities change little and the relevant fiscal policy variable to be analysed is the budget deficits, not the accumulated government debt. More specifically, changes in the size of debt owed by the government are taken to be small enough in the short run relative to the total stock of wealth to have only a modest effect on the permanent saving decisions of households or the investment decisions of businesses. Furthermore, changes in the existing stock of productive capital are thought to be not large enough in the short run to affect noticeably either the level of output or real returns to the factors of production. Long-term expectations in such a world play a limited role in affecting people's behavior. But the economy in the short run can, and frequently does, depart from what is deemed to be its full potential. The government's fiscal and monetary policies, by affecting aggregate demand, can influence the level of economic activity.

Short-run Interest Rate Effects

Large budget deficits are frequently said to raise interest rates. Concern about the effect of deficits on interest rates stems from their unique role in allocating resources among competing uses, in particular between consumption and investment. To say that large deficits contribute to high interest rates is equivalent to saying that large deficits displace or 'crowd out' productive investment. In fact, the blame for all other ills commonly attributed to large deficits stems directly from this assertion. In its simplest form, the argument is that if the government increases its demand for available credit, the price of credit – that is, the interest rate – must go up. An argument often brought against this assertion is that if the increased government borrowing results from a tax cut, then after-tax incomes would rise by the same amount. Some of the increase in incomes will be saved; indeed, all of it will be saved if people expect that increased government debt will have to be serviced by further tax increases. As a result, the borrowing needs of the private sector will decline accordingly, cushioning (or perhaps even preventing altogether) any impact on interest rates.

Another approach, which until fairly recently was readily accepted by a vast majority of economists, is based on standard Keynesian analysis. In its simplest version, Keynesian theory postulates that deficit spending stimulates aggregate demand, thus increasing the demand for money to facilitate a higher level of purchases. If monetary policy remains unchanged, higher demand for money will in most circumstances lead to higher interest rates.

While this theoretical argument appears compelling, a simple test correlating government deficits (as a percentage of GNP) with interest rates would not show that larger deficits are systematically associated with higher interest rates. If anything, the correlation would most likely be negative. There are several reasons for this apparent divergence between the theory and the reality:

- First, interest rates are predominantly determined by the level of economic activity. More specifically, for a given stance of monetary policy, interest rates are determined by the total demand for credit rather than by its particular components. Budget deficits typically increase during periods of economic slack when private demands for credit are low. Since the share of the federal government in total borrowing was until several years ago relatively small, a decrease in private credit demands caused by an economic slowdown was usually much larger in absolute terms than the coincident increase in borrowing by the Treasury. The opposite used to occur during economic recoveries. As a result, total demand for credit tended to be low in periods of economic contraction and high in periods of expansion. The lack of discernible simple correlation between government budget deficits and interest rates is thus not surprising and does not, in itself, demonstrate that there is no connection.
- Second, the theory links deficits to *real* interest rates – that is, observable nominal rates less the *expected* rate of inflation. Consequently, simple tests attempting to find a correlation between deficits and nominal interest rates are not appropriate for confirming or refuting the hypothesis in question. Further, since expected inflation rates and thus real interest rates cannot be measured directly, most attempts at testing the relationship between deficits and real rates are subject to dispute.
- Third, the effects of international trade and capital flows are disregarded in the simple Keynesian model sketched out above. In fact, international capital markets have been perfected over time to such an extent that when a rise in the US budget deficits begins to exert pressure on US capital markets, international capital, some of it owned by Americans, will quickly flow in. These inflows may be induced by such small changes in interest rates that the rate increases are difficult to detect statistically.
- Finally, deliberate efforts by the Federal Reserve to stabilise short-term interest rates may have obscured in the past the linkage between deficits and interest rates. Stable interest rates have diminished in importance as a policy goal since late 1979, suggest-

ing that the recorded pattern of correlation between deficits and interest rates over the last few years could have changed as well.

A variety of empirical studies have attempted to examine the effects of deficits on interest rates in a Keynesian framework embodying one or more modifications of the basic model. Few have uncovered a clear pattern of correlation, let alone a causal link. Most of them – both those that find no relationship as well as those that do – base their conclusions on tenuous evidence. A recent review found that many of their statistical results, whether supporting or denying a relationship between deficits and interest rates, could be reversed by making only minor changes in the statistical relationships tested or in the precise deficit measure used.[2] The overall conclusion is that the relationships are not only exceedingly complex but also may evolve over time in response to such factors as, for example, shifts in monetary policy, major changes in tax laws, or internationalisation of capital markets.

It is extremely difficult to structure models incorporating all these complexities as they change over time, to isolate residual effects of deficits on interest rates, and to test for their quantitative importance. In any case, it is not clear how much relevance studies of past effects have for the current situation. The very size of the recent and projected deficits may have changed the relationship between deficits and interest rates. But large deficits may, under some circumstances, crowd out private productive investment even without having a noticeable impact on interest rates:

- If private investment is very sensitive to interest rates, even a small increase in the rate caused by additional government borrowing may result in significant displacement of private investment. Under such circumstances, harmful effects attributed to large deficits could occur without a discernible shift in interest rates.
- The impact of deficits on interest rates and domestic capital formation is considerably reduced in the presence of international capital flows. If world capital markets were fully integrated and savings generated by foreigners were very large relative to total demand for credit by US residents (inclusive of the government), one would not expect large deficits to have any discernible impact on interest rates. Instead, the flow of foreign capital would result in an appreciation of the US dollar and a resulting current account deficit. This is, indeed, the situation today. As a result of capital

inflows from abroad, upward pressures on US interest rates have been greatly alleviated so that domestic investment does not appear to be 'crowded out'. But the effect of these capital inflows on the value of the US dollar crowds out US export- and import-competing industries by making it more difficult for them to compete internationally. Moreover, it is quite possible that the US deficit is crowding out capital formation in other countries.

Deficits, Savings, and Private Investment

Interest rates ultimately reflect the price or reward paid to savers and serve to allocate saving among alternative uses. The government, because of its insensitivity to interest rates and its unique credit standing, has primary claim on the pool of available credit. The larger the government borrowing requirements are relative to total credit availability, the fiercer will be the competition among private credit users. When the government demands an increasing amount of credit, more private domestic or foreign borrowers are squeezed out of the credit market unless there is a concomitant increase in credit availability. In recent years, government borrowing as a share of domestically generated savings has risen sharply. Net private domestic savings have remained a fairly constant share of GNP since 1950 – around 7.2 per cent (see Table 2.1 and Figure 2.1). But federal deficits, as a percentage of GNP, began to climb in the 1970s, and their climb accelerated dramatically in the 1980s. Even though surpluses of state and local governments rose in the 1970s and 1980s, they did not nearly offset the increase in federal borrowing. The average GNP share of net domestic savings left for domestic private investment declined in the 1970s and dropped precipitously in the early 1980s. Average net private domestic investment as a share of GNP also declined during this same period and only last year rebounded to its historical average, even though the severity of the decline was partly alleviated by increased capital inflows from abroad.

Purely as an accounting matter, larger federal deficits must leave fewer resources available for domestic private investment unless there is a fully compensating increase in private domestic saving, in the budget surpluses of state and local governments, in the inflow of foreign savings, or in all of these together. CBO projects that if policy is not changed, the budget deficits (on a NIPA basis) in the next several years will average 4.6 per cent of GNP, almost three percentage points higher than in the 1970s.[3] This means that available

TABLE 2.1 *Net savings and investment flows as percent of GNP (NIPA basis)*

Period	(1) *Net private domestic savings*	(2) *State and local surplus*	(3) *Federal deficit*	(4) *Net domestic savings available for domestic investment: (1)+(2)–(3)*	(5) *Net private domestic investment*	(6) *Net domestic savings shortfalls (5)–(4) = net foreign investment*
1950–59	7.2	–0.2	–0.1	7.1	7.1	–0.1
1960–69	7.8	0.0	0.3	7.5	7.0	–0.5
1970–79	7.2	0.8	1.8	6.2	6.4	–0.1
1980–84[a]	6.0	1.3	3.9	3.4	4.1	0.7
Average						
1950–84	7.2	0.4	1.1	6.5	6.4	–0.1
1985–90[b]	7.2	1.4	4.6	4.0	6.4	2.4

[a] BEA estimates are used for 1984 state and local surplus and 1984 federal deficit.

[b] Only the federal deficit is a CBO projection. Net private domestic savings and net private domestic investment shares of GNP are assumed for illustrative purposes to be at their averages of the 1970s, while the state and local surplus is assumed to maintain its high estimated share of GNP in 1984. Columns 4 and 6 are calculated from the other figures.

Details may not appear to be consistent with totals because of rounding.

SOURCES: US Department of Commerce, Bureau of Economic Analysis; Congressional Budget Office.

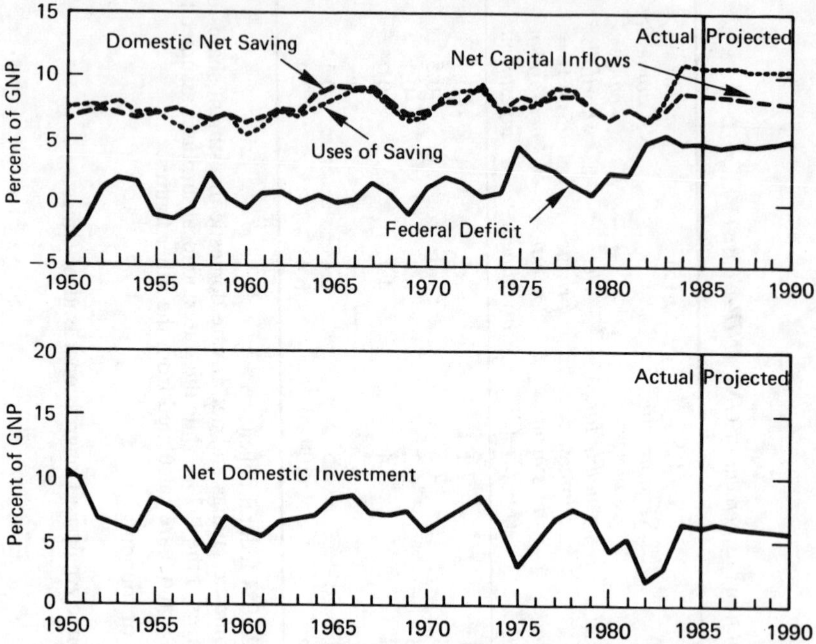

Note: Domestic net saving is net nonfederal domestic saving (columns 1 and 2 in Table 2.1). Uses of saving is net domestic investment plus the federal deficit (columns 3 and 5 in Table 2.1). The difference between domestic net saving and the federal deficit is the amount of domestic savings left for private domestic investment.

SOURCE: Congressional Budget Office.

FIGURE 2.1 *Net savings and investment flows*

savings would have to increase by a comparable amount just to enable net private domestic investment to equal that of the 1970s, when it averaged only 6.4 per cent of GNP. (That level, which was well below the average of the 1960s, is generally believed to be partly responsible for the slower growth in productivity during the 1970s.) Where will these additional savings come from?

Net private domestic savings fell sharply during the early 1980s, in part because of lingering fears of inflation and in part because of the back-to-back recessions in 1980 and in 1981–82. But even if one assumes that net private savings will bounce back sharply and in 1985–90 will match their historical average, and that the combined state and local government surplus will remain at its current historically high level of about 1.4 per cent of GNP, with federal deficits (on an NIPA basis) projected to average 4.6 per cent of GNP over the next six years, the amount of domestically generated savings left for private domestic investment is expected to average only 4.0 per cent of GNP – less than two-thirds of what it was on the average in the 1970s.

Under these conditions, additional savings will be provided by foreigners. If inflows of foreign capital prove to be highly sensitive to interest-rate differentials, a small increase in US interest rates would elicit large capital inflows. These inflows could substantially alleviate the pressures of rising total domestic credit demands, expanded by large deficits, on interest rates. Net private domestic investment could then match the rate that prevailed in the 1970s.

This scenario is broadly consistent with CBO's medium-term projection (see Table 2.1). But capital inflows of the requisite size – about $2\frac{1}{2}$ per cent of GNP – over a period of so many years would be totally unprecedented in modern US history. Leaving aside the question of the long-term consequences of the resulting buildup in US external debt (which will be discussed later), such capital inflows would probably require the continuation of relatively high real interest rates. This is also assumed in the CBO projection. Such capital inflows would keep the external value of the dollar high relative to recent history, further damaging the competitive position of American export- and import-competing industries. Interest-sensitive sectors of the economy engaged in production of nontradeable goods might be largely spared the burden of high government deficits, but only because it would be borne by the foreign trade sector.

At the very least, therefore, the short-run effects of large budget deficits will manifest themselves in sectoral imbalances in the economy. Under the stimulus of government deficits, some sectors of the economy would operate at full capacity while others, especially those competing in foreign trade, would languish.

2.2 PERSISTENT LARGE DEFICITS IN THE LONG RUN

The long-run consequences of persistent large budget deficits are considered by most economists to be far more serious than their short-run consequences. While short-run analysis concentrates on relationships among flows of savings, investment, and consumption, and on the cyclical behavior of the economy, long-run analysis focuses on relationships among gradually changing trends in the real capital stock and production, or, in other words, on secular trends in the economy.

The Danger of Runaway Debt

The most insidious danger of persistent large deficits is that they may result in a runaway accumulation of federal debt. Under current budget policy and under its economic assumptions, CBO does not project such an explosive rise in the federal debt. But it could occur if the economy performed much worse than projected, or if spending was raised or taxes lowered beyond levels implied by current policy.

If federal debt were to grow faster than total net private wealth, an even smaller share of available resources would be left for private capital formation. Should this continue long enough, net private investment could cease entirely and even become negative – the latter implying gradual depletion of the existing stock of physical capital. But such a process could not continue for a long period without provoking political or economic instability.

For a rise in the debt-to-GNP ratio to be nonexplosive – that is, to approach a limit at some point – certain conditions must be satisfied. These conditions are presented in Appendix 2.1 (at the end of the chapter). As a good approximation, the growth path of the debt-to-GNP ratio can be defined in terms of a few key variables:

- The primary deficit – that is, the total (on- and off-budget) deficit, less net interest payments on debt adjusted for Federal Reserve payments to the Treasury;
- The nominal rate of interest on government debt held by the public; and
- The rate of growth of nominal GNP.

The importance of these three variables can be illustrated with a simple arithmetic example. Suppose that the total deficit is exactly equal to the interest bill on the debt – that the primary deficit as defined above is zero. If the average interest rate on the public debt is 10 per cent, the outstanding debt will then grow at a rate of 10 per cent. If the rate of growth of nominal GNP is also 10 per cent, the debt-to-GNP ratio will remain constant.

The differential between the growth rate and interest rate itself is affected by the level of debt relative to GNP. If higher debt levels are associated with higher interest rates, it becomes progressively more difficult to prevent the debt from exploding as it grows and feeds on itself. If the average nominal interest rate on government debt exceeds the rate of growth of nominal GNP in the long run, the debt-to-GNP ratio will rise continuously, unless there is a sufficiently large primary surplus. As the debt burden rises, the size of the interest bill will also grow faster than income. As interest costs become more and more of a burden, the temptation will grow to finance government spending by creating money rather than by borrowing it. If fiscal policies are not changed sufficiently to restore stability, accelerating inflation then becomes almost certain.

If the nominal interest rate is above the rate of growth of nominal GNP and the primary deficit exceeds zero – that is, if government borrowing exceeds interest paid on previously accumulated debt – then the growth of the debt-to-GNP ratio accelerates even faster. A straightforward corollary is that if the primary deficit is constantly growing over time, the process may become explosive even if the nominal interest rate on debt is lower than the rate of growth of nominal GNP. It is only when the growth rate of nominal GNP exceeds the nominal interest rate *and* the primary deficit is not increasing, that the ratio of the overall deficit to GNP is not rising either. In this case the process of debt accumulation is not explosive – that is, the process is stable.[4]

What are the prospects for the key economic variables that determine the stability of the debt-to-GNP ratio between now and 1990? Historical data, together with CBO's projections for coming years, are summarised in Table 2.2 and depicted in Figure 2.2. They show the primary deficit declining just enough to offset rising interest payments on the debt and thus keeping the deficit-to-GNP ratio (counting both the on- and off-budget deficits) virtually constant at about 5.3 per cent between 1986 and 1990. In a strictly formal sense, therefore, the process appears to be sustainable. The projected situation is obviously precarious, however. Interest rates are projected to remain above growth rates through 1990. The projected sustainability of the debt accumulation process is possible only because the primary deficit is declining, which in turn assumes that the economy achieves the projected rates of growth. Should the rate of nominal GNP growth turn out to be lower than projected by CBO in its baseline case, or nominal interest rates higher, or both, the deficit-to-GNP ratio would be a rising one and the debt accumulation process could eventually become explosive. On the other hand, if the

TABLE 2.2 *Primary deficit, interest payments on debt, and total deficit (as a per cent of GNP)*

	Primary deficit[a]	*Interest payments on debt*[b]	*Total deficit*
1950–59	−0.9	1.3	0.4
1960–69	−0.3	1.1	0.8
1970–74	0.1	1.1	1.2
1975–79	1.3	1.3	2.6
1980–84	2.1	2.2	4.3
1985	2.6	3.0	5.6
1986	2.1	3.1	5.2
1987	1.9	3.3	5.2
1988	1.7	3.5	5.1
1989	1.6	3.6	5.2
1990	1.5	3.8	5.3

Note: All figures are on a unified budget basis.
a. The primary deficit is the total federal deficit (on- and off-budget) less net interest payments, adjusted for Federal Reserve payments to the Treasury.
b. Net interest payments less Federal Reserve payments to the Treasury.
SOURCE: Congressional Budget Office.

economy performed better than projected, this could hasten the stabilisation of the debt-to-GNP ratio. But the very fact that, despite the assumption of growth rates exceeding the potential growth of the economy, the debt-to-GNP ratio does not come close to approaching a stable value during the projection period, is evidence of the severe imbalance in US fiscal policy.

2.3 THE CONSEQUENCES OF RAPID DEBT ACCUMULATION

Even if the debt does not grow explosively, the consequences of its long-term rise are serious. Stabilising the deficit-to-GNP ratio at the current high level of above 5 per cent would imply a prolonged buildup of government debt relative to GNP, albeit at a decelerating rate. Such a buildup of debt could have profound long-term effects on the economy and society. These effects, complex and multifaceted, are discussed below under four headings: impairment of capital growth; rising foreign indebtedness; the danger that the Federal

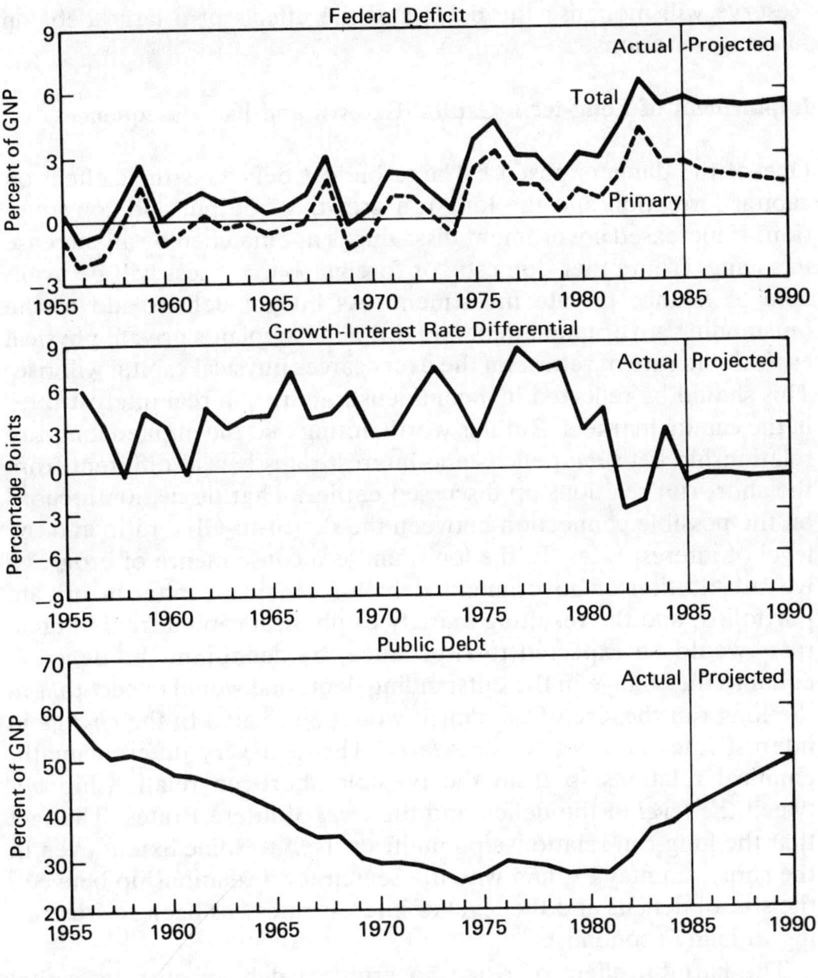

Note: The growth-interest rate differential is the growth rate of GNP, less the effective interest rate on federal debt. The primary deficit is the actual deficit, less net interest payments, adjusted for Federal Reserve payments to the Treasury. Data are for fiscal years.

SOURCE: Congressional Budget Office.

FIGURE 2.2 *Determinants of debt accumulation*

Reserve will monetise the debt; and the effects of a large debt on future generations.

Impairment of Long-term Capital Growth and its Consequences

One of the dangers posed by large budget deficits is their effect on capital formation and the long-run growth of output and consumption. If increased government dissaving is not matched by an increase in savings from other domestic or foreign sources, less will be available to finance private investment. As budget deficits add to the outstanding government debt and this debt supplants private physical capital, the rate of return on the ever scarcer physical capital will rise. This should be reflected in a commensurate rise in real interest rates in the capital markets. But it is worth noting that the implied long-run relationship between deficits and interest rates is very different from the short-run relationship discussed earlier. That discussion focused on the possible connection between the deficit-to-GNP ratio and the level of interest rates. In the long run, as a consequence of progressive substitution of government debt for physical capital in private portfolios, and the resulting scarcity of physical capital, real interest rates would be expected to rise. Since, by definition, the deficit is equal to the change in the outstanding debt, one would expect that in the long run the size of the deficit would be related to the *change* in interest rates and not to their *level*. This is a very different mathematical relationship from the possible short-run relationship between the *level* of the deficit and the *level* of interest rates. The fact that the long-run relationship manifests itself to some extent even in the short run may explain why the search for a relationship between the size of deficits and the level of interest rates has been so frustrating to many economists.[5]

The harmful effect of rising government debt on private capital formation can be shown in other ways, not requiring knowledge of the precise nature and magnitude of the connection between the level of debt and interest rates. A number of economists have reached this same conclusion by focusing on the cumulative impact of budget deficits on the stock of publicly held debt. As a consequence of continuous large deficits, the ratio of publicly held debt to GNP is projected to rise from almost 40 per cent in 1985 to almost 50 per cent in 1990. Benjamin Friedman has argued that the total (government plus private) debt-to-GNP ratio has remained fairly constant since

World War II at about 1.45 – even as components within the total have fluctuated markedly.[6] If history is a guide, this suggests that the projected increase in the federal debt relative to GNP will leave a smaller share of total debt to finance private capital formation. This conclusion is supported by regression equations that show a significant negative impact of the debt-to-GNP ratio on investment. For example, Makin and Sauer have argued that 'deficits sufficiently large to raise the ratio of debt to GNP may serve as a good, exogenous proxy for the expected after-tax rental price of capital.'[7] In other words, expected increases in federal debt relative to GNP may raise expected real interest rates and expected tax burdens. Their empirical findings suggest that a one-percentage-point increase in the change of the debt-to-GNP ratio above what it would be otherwise reduces investment by $75 billion (at an annual rate, in 1984 dollars) spread over five quarters.

A slowing in the pace of net private investment will have an adverse long-run impact on the American economy, both through slowing the growth in the stock of physical capital and by reducing the rate at which new production techniques are introduced. This will slow the rate of productivity and GNP growth, with obvious effects on income and consumption. In addition to these aggregate effects, the decline in the capital-to-output ratio could be expected to slow the growth of real wages of American labour.

Rising Foreign Indebtedness

The rapid buildup in government debt in recent years has been accompanied by an increasing net inflow of international capital. As a result, the difference between foreign asset holdings by Americans and US asset holdings by foreigners has been rapidly declining to the point where the United States has become, or is about to become, a net debtor nation. (See Appendix 2.2 and Table 2.3.) Under CBO's projections, massive inflows of international capital are assumed to continue throughout the rest of the decade if fiscal policy is not changed. These capital inflows and the ensuing increase in net foreign claims on US output are bound to exert a growing influence on the American economy.

Rapid accumulation of external debt need not be accompanied by a similarly rapid rise in foreign holdings of US government securities.[8] The pace of acquisition of government debt by foreign residents

TABLE 2.3 *External financial position of the United States (in billions of dollars)*

	US current account balance	*Balance of payment statistical discrepancy*	*Net international assets*[a]
1970	2.3	–0.3	58.5
1971	–1.4	–9.8	45.5
1972	–5.8	–1.9	37.0
1973	7.1	–2.7	47.9
1974	2.0	–1.5	58.7
1975	18.1	5.9	74.2
1976	4.2	10.5	83.6
1977	–14.5	–2.0	72.7
1978	–15.4	12.5	76.1
1979	–1.0	25.4	94.5
1980	1.9	25.0	106.1
1981	6.3	22.3	143.1
1982	–9.2	32.9	149.5
1983	–41.6	9.3	106.0
	Projected		
1984	–103.0	0	3.0
1985	–109.0	0	–106.0
1986	–130.0	0	–236.0

a. Data for 1984 to 1986 are based on CBO estimates and projections of the current account balance.

SOURCES: US Department of Commerce, Bureau of Economic Analysis; Congressional Budget Office.

is, however, irrelevant for the task of assessing the connection between the buildup in government debt and an increase in the country's total external indebtedness.

First, private debt (and other private assets) are fairly good substitutes for government securities. To the extent that foreigners buy private US assets, they release domestic savings for purchases of government debt – domestic savings that otherwise would have been used to finance private domestic investment. If this pattern continued long enough, foreigners would end up with the bulk of their dollar-denominated assets in the form of claims on US physical capital while the wealth of Americans would increasingly consist of government securities.

Second, the dominant participants in the international capital markets are US-based institutions with geographically diversified assets and liabilities. In recent years those institutions have chosen to curtail their investments abroad and invest more at home. Thus, while gross purchases of US assets by foreigners appear to have been relatively modest, they were accompanied by disinvestment overseas by US residents. On a net transactions basis, capital inflows (abstracting from errors and omissions) are – by definition – equal to US current account deficits and – also by definition – to the increase in US net external indebtedness.

If the decumulation of US assets abroad coincided with additional investment of equal magnitude at home, then total wealth of US residents would remain unchanged even though its location would be shifting from overseas to the United States. To the extent, however, that the depletion of American-owned assets abroad simply allows temporary maintenance of current consumption in the United States at an otherwise unsustainable level, the foreign component of American-owned wealth will shrink without a matching increase in its US-located component.

To the extent that rising government debt contributes to higher real rates of return in this country, one would expect dollar-denominated assets to become more and more attractive relative to assets denominated in other currencies. Indeed, statistical estimates of the responsiveness of international capital flows to interest rates – although it varies over time – indicate that the differential between US and foreign interest rates is an important determinant of capital flows.[9]

By providing an additional source of funds to the US economy, net capital inflows induced by federal deficits tend to make domestic interest rates lower than they would be otherwise. Thus, it is most likely that domestic interest rates are higher than they would be in the absence of persistent large government deficits, but are lower than they would be if sources of foreign capital were not available. On the other hand, by allowing a net export deficit, net capital inflows tend to lower the level of domestic output. In fact, much of the economic stimulus from federal deficits may eventually be transferred abroad through the trade effects of real exchange-rate appreciation induced by capital flows.[10]

Since capital inflows lower interest rates and also finance an import surplus, they make more resources available to the United States. If the additional resources are used for investment capable of generating returns exceeding the real rate of interest paid on foreign debt, the United States, by attracting capital from abroad, where the expected real return on investment is presumably lower, can be said to contribute to its own and other countries' well-being, just as it did in the nineteenth century when large capital inflows helped finance the development of US canals and railroads. But if current capital inflows serve only to sustain more or less normal levels of US net investment while domestic savings are drained off to finance additional consumption through budget deficits, then the United States is not generating sufficient additional production to pay the interest and dividends on the growing foreign debt.

A question arises as to how long and to what extent this process can be sustained. If it is to continue, holdings of dollar assets by foreigners must grow very rapidly, perhaps further increasing as a share of their total wealth. Ultimately, it is likely that the amount of dollar assets in international portfolios would become too large relative to the total wealth of foreigners. In order to restore the desired composition of their portfolios, international investors might deny additional funds to US borrowers except at higher interest rates. As capital inflows slowed, or ceased entirely, domestic interest rates could rise, perhaps sharply, and growth in the federal debt could become explosive.

Eventually, the dollar would have to depreciate sufficiently to allow a trade surplus large enough to finance interest and amortisation payments on the external debt. Domestic export- and import-competing industries, which had already undergone contraction in response to real appreciation of the dollar, would then face a second round of adjustment costs as they expanded in response to declining real dollar exchange rates. Since domestic spending would have to fall below domestic output, it is quite possible that consumption *per capita* would shrink.

Before this point was reached, foreign capital inflows might continue for a very long time and on a massive scale. Americans would enjoy increased purchasing power over foreign goods and services. But they would be borrowing from future generations through the government deficit, and through the export deficit as well. As the rest of the world accumulated a mass of claims against the United States, the ratio of net external debt to GNP could become very large, much as it did for major Third World borrowers during the late 1970s and early 1980s. Growing foreign claims would mean that an increasing portion of US productive capacity would be owned by foreign residents, and more and more of the US labour force would be working for foreign owners of US capital.

While the above analysis has developed a link between US budget deficits and net inflows of international capital, other factors may also contribute to inflows. The relative political stability of the United States, and sluggish economies in other countries, make the United States relatively attractive to investors. A more prudent US policy might so enhance investor confidence in the long-term health of the US economy that capital inflows would increase as US deficits fell. If that happened, United States interest rates could be expected to fall dramatically, and a higher proportion of US plus foreign savings would be invested in increasing productive capacities.

Debt Monetisation

Another danger of persistent large deficits and resulting high debt levels is that the Federal Reserve migh decide to step up its acquisition of government debt. This is most likely to happen if the central bank placed a high priority on stabilising interest rates. If the deficits began to push up interest rates, the Federal Reserve might seek to relieve some of the pressure by increasing its holdings of government debt. Substantial additions to its portfolio would raise the monetary base and the money stock above the levels that would obtain otherwise, and could ultimately lead to more rapid inflation. Conversely, if the Federal Reserve downgraded the goal of interest rate stability and put greater importance on maintaining a constant growth rate of the money supply, it would, by definition, be attempting to rule out the possibility of monetisation.

This question about the Federal Reserve's behaviour has been subjected to a number of empirical tests, the conclusions of which, as might be expected, are mixed. Some economists believe they have found consistent and relatively stable tendencies to monetise government debt, while others believe that no such tendencies can be uncovered.

The charts in Figure 2.3 contain historical data on the ratio of the monetary base to publicly held government debt, and on the ratio of changes in the base to deficits. They suggest that monetisation rose sharply from the early 1960s through the middle of the 1970s, but has dropped just as sharply since that time (see the upper panel of Figure 2.3). This decline in debt monetisation need not indicate that future

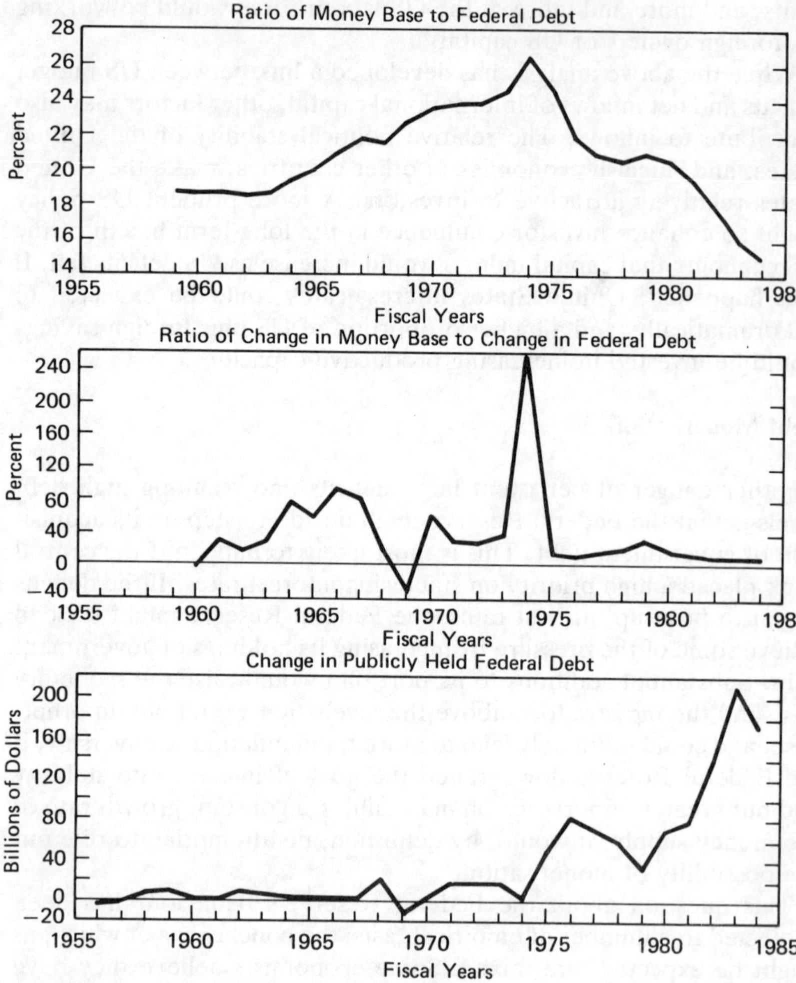

Note: Data on the monetary base are for the last month of the fiscal year, not seasonally adjusted. Data on total publicly held government debt, including federal agency debt, are for the end of the fiscal year, not seasonally adjusted.

SOURCE: Federal Reserve Board.

FIGURE 2.3 *Selected measures of federal debt monetisation*

deficits may not be inflationary. The decline in the ratio of the monetary base to debt has occurred concomitantly with a precipitous increase in government debt levels, so that, even at the lower monetisation rates, the amount of debt being monetised is large in absolute terms. For example, if the deficits projected by CBO for the years 1985–90 were monetised at the 1984 historical rate, the addition to the stock of debt of almost $1.5 trillion would contribute about $130 billion to the monetary base. Assuming a money multiplier of 2.8 – about the 1984 average – the money supply would expand by about $364 billion, for an average growth rate over the period of 9.0 per cent.[11]

Since historical extrapolations are sometimes biased by aberrations in data occurring in the most recent periods, CBO also re-estimated an equation formulated by Hamburger and Zwick relating money growth to deficits.[12] Forecasts of money growth using this re-estimated equation and CBO deficit and price projections generated somewhat lower growth rates than the historical extrapolation – 8 per cent to $8\frac{1}{2}$ per cent annually over the same period. Thus this forecast calls for money growth above the Federal Reserve's preliminary M1 target for 1985 of 4 per cent to 7 per cent. In other words, by announcing such a target, the central bank is, in effect, stating that it plans a lower degree of monetisation than may have occurred in the past.

Even if it were not implicitly restricted by its desire to achieve a money growth target, some evidence suggests a lower tendency to monetise when deficits are large – that is, the Federal Reserve appears to be less willing to monetise the same proportion of a large increment of debt than it is of a small increment. Hamburger and Zwick and the CBO economists all noticed that the propensity to monetise was lower than suggested by this equation during 1975 and 1976 – years of excessively large deficits. If this holds in the future, estimates of money growth from the equation reported above may overstate the monetisation pressures. On the other hand, the deficits in 1975 and 1976 may have been viewed as more transitory than those of the 1980s. It is conceivable that persistently large deficits and growing debt levels in the 1980s, in conjunction with strong private-sector credit demands, may force the Federal Reserve into monetising more of the debt than in the past. In any event, the size of projected deficits will continue to pose problems for a monetary policy concerned with controlling inflation while maintaining stable interest rates.

Many do not accept the above evidence of an automatic tendency to monetise in the past. Technically, monetisation does not have to occur. If it did occur in the past, it need not continue since the Federal Reserve can change its goals and operating procedures – as it has in the past.

The Issue of Intergenerational Fairness

Whether the long-term consequences discussed above take the form of slower long-run capital growth per worker, the accumulation of foreign claims on US output, or the reduction in the value of private liquid wealth through inflation, they all amount to intertemporal shifts in consumption between the present and future generations.

The dissaving represented by the budget deficit allows present consumption to rise at the expense of future consumption. Although there is considerable uncertainty as to the empirical magnitudes involved, two related analytic approaches have been pursued in an effort to estimate them. The first approach attempts to calculate the present value of the consumption loss that arises as a result of current budget policy. Rough estimates of the effect of an increased federal debt-to-GNP ratio on private investment are made and then the impact of this investment shortfall on future consumption is gauged. Calculations by John Makin indicate that the rise in the debt-to-GNP ratio occurring or projected to occur in the 1979 to 1989 period leads to consumption losses of approximately $880 billion (in 1984 dollars).[13] This is not a statement that consumption in the 1979 to 1989 period is lowered by the rise in the debt-to-GNP ratio. Rather, it is a measure of a difference between two long-run consumption streams, one that would occur under present circumstances and another that would have occurred in the absence of enlarged budget deficits in 1979–89.

An alternative approach pursued by Edward Gramlich attempts to determine the period of time over which the large deficits of the 1980s can be expected to raise present consumption above the path that would have occurred if the deficit-to-GNP ratio had stayed more in line with its levels in the 1970s.[14] Here the goal is not to value present consumption gains against future losses. Rather, Gramlich examines the horizon over which the direct increase in consumption afforded by the budget deficits is great enough to outweigh the losses to future consumption brought by the accompanying shortfall of investment. Depending on the particular assumptions employed, his results suggest that consumption would not fall below the levels that would have been achieved with smaller deficits for a period from 12 to 25 years.

These results indicate that any net increases in *per capita* consumption that might be brought about by deficit reductions would lie many years into the future, but would grow at an increasing rate. Setting aside all the other arguments against running large deficits over many years, a question arises as to the effects of deficit reductions on the consumption levels of later generations.[15] Proponents of deficit cuts argue that since most future generations are unrepresented in this debate, special measures must be taken to give fair consideration to their interests.

Economic theory cannot by itself determine a 'fair' distribution of consumption between present and future generations. Such determination involves, among other things, a political value judgment. Economists have, however, explored the implications of one explicit value judgment known as the 'golden rule'. This would be a saving rate (that is, a percentage of GNP devoted to saving) that would maximise the permanent *per-capita* consumption of all generations.[16] As long as all generations followed the rule and saved the same percentage of GNP (and the consumption levels enjoyed by different generations were valued equally, without discounting future consumption), the result would be intergenerationally 'neutral' or 'fair'. Rough calculations based on the golden rule suggest that Americans at present appear to be dissaving or consuming too much to be 'fair' in this sense. This would imply that saving should be increased. Reducing the deficit would be one way of achieving this goal.[17]

Such analyses provide little practical guidance to policy, however, because they require a multitude of assumptions, not all of which would be accepted by most observers. For example, there is no good reason other than the appeal of simplicity, to postulate a saving rate that is constant over time. Since most analysts expect future generations to enjoy higher standards of living than the present one, it might be argued that people living today should consume a larger share of their income in order to make present and future consumption levels more nearly equal. But even this would not justify unlimited deficits. Aside from the stability problem discussed earlier, there is a limit – albeit difficult to determine – to how much consumption should be shifted forward in time. Certainly, no principle of equity would justify making future generations worse off than the present one.

2.4 GOALS FOR DEFICIT POLICY

What ought to be the goals of a policy aimed at reducing the size of federal deficits? Many different proposals have been put forward, but most can be grouped into four categories. Some would try to set the deficit or debt at a particular level. Most often this approach aims at balancing the budget (either continuously or over the course of the business cycle) or stabilising the debt relative to GNP. A second, somewhat less stringent approach would allow budget deficits during recessions, but would require a balanced structural budget (the budget computed as 'though' some high level of employment obtained). A third category of proposals would use deficits to maximise social welfare over the long term – for example, maximising long-run consumption. A fourth category would tolerate deficits that serve to reduce inefficiencies associated with frequent changes in tax rates.

A Balanced Budget or a Stable Debt Level

The most common proposal involves balancing the budget. It is based not so much on economic arguments as on the feeling that government spending should be disciplined by restraining it to the level of tax receipts.[18] This view does not recognise any role for the federal government in stabilising the economy.

A related but less restrictive approach would balance the budget over the course of the business cycle. It would allow deficits during periods of economic slack, provided that they were offset by surpluses during economic booms. Thus, unlike the balanced budget rule, this norm does not force the budget to be procyclical in its effect on the economy.[19] It resembles a balanced budget norm, however, in that it incorporates the popular view that over time the federal government should not incur debt by allowing federal spending to outstrip federal revenues, on average.

Proponents of stabilising the debt-to-GNP ratio are willing to tolerate some long-term deficit spending. They believe that federal debt can be absorbed without raising interest rates so long as it does not grow faster than GNP. If interest rates were constant, this policy norm would ensure that the federal interest bill relative to GNP would also remain constant. Proposals to stabilise the debt-to-GNP ratio do not state specifically at what level the target should be set. If it was set much higher than the actual ratio at any given time, this would allow a series of growing deficits for some time. Conversely, if the selected ratio was lower than the actual one, declining deficits (relative to GNP) or possibly even budget surpluses would be required to reach the policy goal. Moreover, even if everyone agreed on the desired debt-to-GNP ratio, this policy rule – like other norms discussed here – would not deal with the question of time. The length of time over which the budget was to be brought into balance, or the debt-to-GNP ratio stabilised, would have a considerable effect on the size of deficits in the interim.

A Balanced Structural Budget

A second class of proposals is based on the idea that the federal budget should provide passive (nondiscretionary) fiscal stimulus and restraint. For example, policymakers might seek to maintain a balanced structural deficit – that is, a balanced budget standardised at a specific rate of unemployment. The rate of unemployment usually suggested is the lowest rate of unemployment consistent with a constant rate of inflation (in the absence of supply shocks). Although highly uncertain, estimates of the 'nonaccelerating inflation rate of unemployment' (NAIRU) are generally about 6 per cent to $6\frac{1}{2}$ per cent.[20]

Balancing the structural deficit would mean that the actual budget would be in deficit when the unemployment rate exceeded the NAIRU, in surplus when the rate of unemployment was below the NAIRU, and in balance when the economy was at the NAIRU. Such a policy would allow cyclical changes in revenues and outlays to act as automatic stabilisers of output and employment in time of economic slack, and as automatic stabilisers of interest rates, exchange rates, and inflation when economic resources are fully employed.[21] At the same time, it would rule out all other discretionary fiscal actions by the government designed to stabilise the economy.

Balancing the structural budget would not be equivalent to balancing the budget over the course of the business cycle. The reason is that, on average, the unemployment rate observed in the economy has been higher than most estimates of the NAIRU. As a result, the nominal federal debt would grow over time because the deficits incurred when the unemployment rate exceeded the NAIRU would cumulate to a larger sum than the surpluses incurred when the unemployment rate was below the NAIRU. In contrast, a policy that balanced the budget over the course of the business cycle would not result in long-run increases in the federal debt, because the deficits

TABLE 2.4 *Alternative measures of the federal deficit (in fiscal years and billions of dollars)*

	1984	*1985*	*1986*	*1987*	*1988*	*1989*	*1990*
Unified budget deficit	175	203[d]	206	225	240	266	290
Off-budget outlays	10	11	9	8	8	6	6
Total deficit	185	214	215	233	249	272	296
Standardised-employment deficit[a b]	121	171[d]	177	199	221	251	282
Middle-expansion deficit[a c]	173	227[d]	237	263	290	324	361
Publicly held federal debt	1313	1526	1740	1972	2220	2490	2786
Per cent of GNP	36.7	39.6	41.8	44.0	46.0	47.9	49.7

a. Includes off-budget outlays.
b. Standardised at 6 per cent unemployment.
c. The middle-expansion deficit is a budget measure that is standardised at trend levels of output and unemployment rates. Its size is much larger than the structural deficit measured at 6 per cent unemployment, but its *change* from one period to the next is similar in magnitude. For a discussion of the middle-expansion deficit, see Frank de Leeuw and Thomas M. Holloway, 'Cyclical Adjustment of the Federal Budget and Federal Debt', *Survey of Current Business*, vol. 63, no. 12 (December 1983), pp. 25–40. See also Congressional Budget Office, *The Economic Outlook* (February 1984), Appendix B.
d. Includes \$13 billion in budget outlays arising from HUD purchases of federally guaranteed notes issued by housing authorities. Such a financial transaction would not be included in a measure of the structural deficit reported on an NIPA basis, but CBO has included it because the CBO estimate is reported on a unified budget basis.

SOURCE: Congressional Budget Office.

that generate debt during periods of economic slack would be offset by debt-reducing surpluses during periods of below-average unemployment.

The CBO projects the structural deficit (standardised at 6 per cent unemployment) as rising from \$171 billion in 1985 to \$282 billion by 1990 (see Table 2.4). In comparison, the middle-expansion deficit – the deficit standardised at trend rates of unemployment – rises from \$227 billion to \$361 billion during the projection period. Balancing the budget over the course of the business cycle (a balanced middle-expansion deficit) would entail substantially more deficit reduction than balancing the budget at a 6 per cent rate of unemployment.[22]

Deficits to Maximise Per Capita Consumption

A third norm for guiding deficit choices would be maximising domestic *per capita* consumption now and in the future. Deficits increase current consumption as long as they finance government spending on consumption rather than on public investment, as is largerly true in the United States now. But they may reduce future consumption if they crowd out private investment in productive capital.

Reductions in potential output that are caused by budget deficits can be roughly estimated by comparing the present outlook with an alternative in which the structural deficit is reduced in 1985 and all later years to the proportion of potential GNP that it represented during the 1970s. Assuming that all private savings freed by cutting the deficit would be used to increase net capital formation implies that potential GNP in 1986 (the GNP level that would occur at high levels of employment) would be perhaps 0.1 per cent or roughly $4 billion higher than it would otherwise be (in 1984 dollars). By 1990, these increases would grow to roughly 0.7 per cent or $31 billion, and by 1999, to perhaps 2.0 per cent of potential GNP.[23] These increases in potential GNP would raise potential consumption correspondingly.

Other assumptions would no doubt yield very different magnitudes of permanent consumption losses associated with recent and projected budget deficits. The key issue, however, is that in principle there exists a particular rate of saving by society as a whole, and by the government in particular, that maximises the value of future consumption.

As mentioned earlier in this chapter, economists have attempted to calculate this consumption-maximising saving rate and the deficit that it implies. Their conclusions are that there may be a particular 'golden rule' saving rate that, if maintained permanently, would maximise consumption for all generations. The specifics of such 'golden rule' calculations should not be taken too literally, since the simplified analysis that they use is strictly valid only for the very long run and fails to take account of certain important features of the economy. One such feature is the presence of net flows of saving between the United States and other countries. If net inflows of foreign saving to the United States increase when deficits do, as has happened recently, then a particular domestic saving rate does not have precisely the same implications for future consumption as it has in the 'golden rule' analysis. The reason for this is that capital inflows make it possible to enjoy higher current consumption and higher investment at the same time. While 'golden rule' calculations taking account of the availability of foreign saving for domestic capital formation are not available as yet, many analysts are convinced that the present rate of total saving in the United States is not sufficient to maximise living standards of Americans in the long run.

Deficits to Smooth Tax Rates Over Time

The final category of deficit policy views the appropriate size of the deficit in terms of the contribution that deficits can make to minimising the economic inefficiency (waste) associated with frequent changes in tax rates. According to public finance theory, frequent changes in tax rates are inefficient because they induce people to alter the timing of their economic activities (work, consumption, investment, and so forth) so as to reduce their tax liabilities.[24] Consequently, the government should set the level of tax rates in the light of long-run normal revenue needs, and should not alter these tax rates to avoid temporary deficits (or surpluses). In other words, deficits should be allowed to vary in order to maintain expected constancy in tax rates.

Based on this view of efficient tax policy, the tax-smoothing size of the *real* federal deficit would be determined by the state of the economy and by the amount of abnormal real federal spending. The tax-smoothing size of the *nominal* deficit would depend on these same factors and on the rate of inflation:

- During recessions and other periods of economic slack, federal revenues are lowered by high rates of unemployment that depress the federal tax base. The resulting (temporary) deficits, however, can be viewed as contributing to economic efficiency in that they allow the government to avoid a temporary increase in tax rates. If the government were to raise tax rates in order to stabilise revenues during such periods, the temporary increase in tax rates would induce people to shift their economic activities into periods of normal (lower) tax rates. This shifting of economic activity would be a waste of economic resources, since it would not have occurred in the absence of the change in tax rates.
- Deficits can also contribute to economic efficiency when there is an abnormally large amount of real federal spending, as in time of war when military needs must be met. If the government were to raise

tax rates to finance its unusual spending requirements, it would alter the after-tax costs and returns from economic activity in one period compared to another, and thus would distort the timing of economic activity.

- Finally, given that the tax-smoothing size of the *real* federal deficit depends on real factors such as the degree of economic slack and the extent of unusual real federal spending, it is not affected by the rate of inflation. The tax-smoothing size of the *nominal* deficit, however, rises proportionally with the rate of inflation.

Deficit Reductions Required to Meet the Norms

The deficits being projected by CBO, assuming that current policies continue, are far larger than those implied by the various norms discussed above. But the differences vary considerably and, in addition, are very sensitive to changes in economic assumptions underlying the computations. In fiscal year 1988 – the last year to be covered by the fiscal year 1986 budget resolution – the projected deficit would have to be reduced by $249 billion to balance the total budget and by $221 billion to eliminate the total structural deficit. In order to keep the debt-to-GNP ratio in fiscal year 1988 at the level of the preceding fiscal year, the budget deficit in 1988 would have to be reduced by $95 billion dollars from the level projected by CBO. The projected baseline deficits also appear too large to satisfy the consumption-maximising and tax-smoothing criteria, although these are much more difficult to estimate. Economic theory alone cannot determine which target is most appropriate. But there is clearly a need for measures to reduce the deficit substantially irrespective of which one of the discussed policy norms is chosen.

2.5 EFFECTS AND TIMING OF DEFICIT REDUCING MEASURES

If deficits are reduced significantly, the country will escape the dangers of rapidly mounting federal debt described earlier in this chapter even if the economy performs less well than projected by CBO over the next six years. Some argue, however, that efforts to reduce the deficit rapidly could have a contractionary impact on the economy. This worry may gain intensity if the economy exhibits symptoms of weakness. Given the magnitude and timing of the deficit reduction being contemplated, is this worry legitimate?

Most economists believe that large reductions in the deficit are likely to have some adverse impact in the short run.[25] The negative effects would clearly be less if deficit reductions are phased in gradually and if their impact on aggregate demand occurred when the economy was growing very rapidly, as it was, for example in, the first half of 1984. It is extremely difficult, however, to time efforts aimed at deficit reduction so that they offset the vicissitudes of the economic cycle. In practice, there is often a lag of several months between the enactment of tax or spending laws and their effects on receipts and outlays, and still another lag between changes in government outlays or receipts and resulting private spending decisions. Thus, deficit-reducing measures undertaken in mid-1985 would be unlikely to have a major direct impact on the economy until at least 1986, and the most important effects might come even later. Since the relevant time lags span a large portion of the duration of a typical business cycle, immediate signs of economic weakness might not be very relevant to the policy decision. Policy measures taken during the contraction phase of a cycle may not have an impact until the economy had already reversed direction of its own accord. These lags suggest that deficit-reducing plans should not be based on prevailing economic conditions but rather on the longer-term outlook, uncertain as it may be.

The contractionary effect of deficit reduction would be partly cushioned by other factors. Curtailment of the Treasury's borrowing needs would reduce upward pressure on interest rates and stimulate interest-sensitive domestic expenditure. According to some economic theories, such contractionary effects could be completely offset very quickly. The dollar would also probably depreciate, which in time would strengthen net exports. Moreover, if the economy seemed about to react adversely in the short run to a change in fiscal policy, the Federal Reserve could shift to a somewhat more expansionary monetary policy.

A credible attack on the deficit problem should also improve expectations in the financial markets and make longer-term investments more attractive. This would further offset any short-run adjustment costs imposed by deficit reductions.

APPENDIX 2.1 DEFICIT AND DEBT DYNAMICS

The issue of debt dynamics and the possibility of instability, implying that the debt-to-GNP ratio could grow without bound, can be illustrated by the following simple example. It will turn out that the issue will depend critically on the values of two measures that will be explained below: the *primary surplus* and the *growth-interest differential*.

Suppose for simplicity that GNP grows at a constant rate, n, and that the rate of interest on government debt is also a constant, i. By definition, the change in debt, D, is the deficit, which is given by the excess of expenditures, E, over taxes, T. This relation can be written:

$$D - D_{-1} = E - T, \qquad (1)$$

where D and D_{-1} represent the debt at the end of the current and previous periods, respectively, so that $(D - D_{-1})$ is the change in debt during the period (that is, the deficit).

Now consider that some expenditures represent interest payments on the debt outstanding at the end of the previous period. Equation (1) can be rewritten as:

$$D - D_{-1} = E' - T + iD_{-1}, \qquad (2)$$

where E' represents expenditures excluding the service on outstanding debt, given by iD_{-1}. For convenience, call $(E' - T)$ the *primary deficit* and denote it as X, so that:

$$D - D_{-1} = X + iD_{-1}. \qquad (3)$$

Now let Y denote GNP and assume that the primary deficit-to-GNP ratio is a constant given by x. Dividing equation (3) through by Y and remembering that Y always equals $(1 + n)\ Y_{-1}$ because the growth rate, n, is assumed constant, we can derive a difference equation for the debt-to-GNP ratio, d:

$$d = x + (1 + i)\ d_{-1}/(1 + n). \qquad (4)$$

For convenience, approximate $(1 + i)/(1 + n)$ to $(1 + \mathrm{i} - n)$. Then the solution of this equation that gives the value of d_t, the debt-to-GNP ratio t periods after starting from an initial value of d_0, is given by:

$$d_t = x/(n-i) + (d_0 - x/(n-i))\ (1 + i - n)^t.$$

If n is greater than i, the *growth-interest differential*, $(n-i)$, is positive, so $(1 + i - n)$ is a fraction less than one. Therefore, as t grows with the passage of time, $(1 + \mathrm{i} - \mathrm{n})^t$ shrinks toward zero, so the process is stable and d tends toward the value given by $x/(n - i)$ no matter what the value of d_0. On the other hand, if i is greater than n, the growth-interest differential is negative and $(1 + i - n)$ is greater than one. Thus, as t grows $(1 + i - n)^t$ also grows. In this case the process is unstable, and the only way to keep d from growing without limit is to choose from the start a primary *surplus* so that the value of $x/(n - i)$ is equal to the initial debt, d_0. This would keep d from either rising or falling.

APPENDIX 2.2 IS THE UNITED STATES AN INTERNATIONAL DEBTOR?

When the United States imports more goods and services than it exports, it runs a current account deficit that is paid by transferring financial claims to foreigners. Whether this financing takes the form of reducing US claims on foreigners or of increasing foreign claims on the United States, the result is a reduction in the US international asset position. As shown in Table 2.3, US current account deficits have totalled over $150 billion in the last three years. At the same time, net US holdings of foreign assets have declined markedly. If these holdings at the end of 1983 were reduced by the amount of the estimated 1984 current account deficit of approximately $100 billion, the United States would currently be very close to becoming a net debtor. The international investment position, however, is affected by changes in the value of assets as well as by the capital flows that finance current account deficits. Movements in interest rates affect the valuation of bond portfolios just as exchange rate changes have an impact on the dollar value of foreign assets. These valuation effects can be significant.

Yet even with these adjustments, the reported net foreign investment position of the United States may not accurately reflect the 'true' position. There are two sources of potentially large errors. The first arises from sizable statistical discrepancies in the international transactions data. Rather than attempting to apportion the discrepancy between capital transactions on the one hand and net exports of goods and non-factor services on the other, the Commerce Department assumes that all the errors arise in the current account. The polar opposite assumption would be that the statistical discrepancy arises solely from capital transactions and investment income flows. That could make the US net investment position significantly smaller. This raises the possibility that the United States may have already become a debtor nation.

The second problem for an accurate assessment of the investment position is that direct investment – ownership of a firm's equity in which the ownership share exceeds 10 per cent – is carried at historical value. Given the history of inflation here and abroad and the fact that the US net direct investment position was until recently positive and large, valuation on a historical basis may understate the actual US international investment position. Valuation of the direct investment portion on a replacement cost basis taking account of the effect of inflation on the value of assets is likely to produce estimates of the US net investment position much higher than officially reported.

Given these uncertainties of measurement, it is impossible to determine whether the United States is at present a net debtor. But the very large projected current account deficits point to a substantial worsening of the US net investment position in the years to come.

NOTES

1. Needless to say, the long run is a chain of overlapping short runs, and therefore short-run consequences can have an impact on the nation's long-run economic health. The distinction between the short run and the long run is useful, however, as a way of distinguishing between the effects of large deficits on the cyclical behavior of the economy and their effects on long-term economic trends.
2. See James R. Barth, George Iden, & Frank S. Russek, 'Do Federal Deficits Really Matter?' *Contemporary Policy Issues* (September 1984), p. 80.
3. Budget deficit numbers cited here and displayed in Table 2.1 are on a National Income and Product Accounts (NIPA) basis. The NIPA measure of the federal deficit is frequently used for economic analysis. Its construction differs from the unified budget deficit in four aspects: timing of transactions, netting and grossing of receipts against spending, treatment of lending activities, and coverage. For a discussion of these differences, see Congressional Budget Office, *Baseline Budget Projections for Fiscal Years 1985–1989* (February 1984).
4. Stability of a dynamic process, such as debt accumulation, refers strictly to a set of characteristics allowing it to converge toward a finite value. Stability in this context does not mean that the path of debt accumulation need be smooth. Neither does the term 'stability' rule out fluctuations in economic aggregates.
5. In the short run, a given level of deficit (relative to GNP) can be associated with either a falling or rising debt-to-GNP ratio. For example, from fiscal year 1983 to 1984 the deficit-to-GNP ratio fell but the debt-to-GNP ratio rose significantly. According to CBO projections, however, both ratios will rise between fiscal years 1984 and 1985.
6. Benjamin M. Friedman, 'Implications of the Government Deficit for US Capital Formation,' *The Economics of Large Government Deficits*, Federal Reserve Bank of Boston (1984).
7. John H. Makin & Raymond D. Sauer, 'The Effect of Debt Accumulation on Capital Formation,' *American Enterprise Institute*, Occasional Papers no. 1 (November 1984), p. 2.
8. In fact, foreign holdings of US government debt have risen quite slowly in recent years. (Foreign purchases of nongovernment US assets have also been rising more moderately than the widening of the current account deficit would lead one to expect.)
9. This is particularly true of portfolio investment flows, and is probably true of direct investment flows as well, because US direct investment flows frequently reflect borrowing in the Eurobond market by US companies through their foreign affiliates.
10. In the extreme, if international capital were sufficiently mobile and if the American economy were sufficiently small relative to the rest of the world (which is demonstrably not the case), the entire fiscal stimulus would be transferred abroad by net capital inflows; both the rate of interest and the level of aggregate output would be the same as in the absence of the internal and external deficits.

11. The money multiplier is the ratio of the money stock to the monetary base and is meant to describe the relationship between these two variables.
12. Michael J. Hamburger & Burton Zwick, 'Deficits, Money and Inflation,' *Journal of Monetary Economics*, vol. 7, no. 1 (1981), pp. 141–50.
13. John H. Makin, 'The Effects of Government Deficits on Capital Formation,' *Contemporary Economic Problems 1985: The Economy in Deficit*, American Enterprise Institute for Public Policy Research, Washington, D.C. (forthcoming).
14. Edward M. Gramlich, 'How Bad are the Large Deficits?', in Gregory B. Mills & John L. Palmer (eds), *Federal Budget Policy in the 1980s*, The Urban Institute Press (1984).
15. This view of the consumption implications of deficit reducing is potentially misleading, however, because much of what the federal government provides through deficit spending also represents consumption for society. Cutting the deficit would reduce government provided consumption enough to offset any gains in private consumption for some time. Whether citizens value their individual consumption and collective government-provided consumption equally is another question.
16. Edmund S. Phelps, 'The Golden Rule of Accumulation: A Fable for Growthmen,' *The American Economic Review*, vol. 51, no. 4 (1961), pp. 638–43.
17. Reducing the deficit may not increase consumption for later generations if individuals today neutralize the effects of decreased borrowing by the government. For example, individuals may now be saving extra money to help their descendants pay interest and principal on the national debt. If the deficit were reduced, such extra saving might also be reduced. See Robert J. Barro, 'Are Government Bonds Net Wealth?', *Journal of Political Economy*, vol. 82, no. 6 (1974), pp. 1095–118.
18. Unless a desired level of taxation is specified, balancing the budget does not directly deal with the issue of what is the appropriate size of the federal sector. The reason is that the budget can be balanced with federal outlays and revenues representing large or small shares of GNP.
19. Such a rule has little advantage over a strict budget balancing rule for those who assume that fiscal policy has little short-run impact on the economy. Furthermore, neither of the two rules allows for borrowing to finance public investment in capital assets.
20. See note 8.
21. It has been argued that instead of balancing the structural deficit, an optimal policy would be to maintain a structural budget *surplus*. The rationale is that government surpluses could offset any reduction in private saving resulting from income taxation. Capital accumulation could then follow the path that would be realized in the absence of income taxes. See Martin J. Bailey, 'The Optimal Full-Employment Surplus,' *Journal of Political Economy*, vol. 80, no. 4 (1972) pp. 649–61.
22. If productivity growth was stronger than expected, federal revenues measured at any rate of unemployment would be greater, and thus the amount of deficit reductions needed to balance the structural deficit at 6 per cent would be less.

23. These calculations were made using the growth model described by Edward Gramlich in Table 5, Version A of 'How Bad Are the Large Deficits?' in Gregory B. Mills & John L. Palmer (eds), *Federal Budget Policy in the 1980s* (The Urban Institute Press, 1984), pp. 43–68.
24. For a discussion of this theory, see Robert J. Barro, 'On the Determination of the Public Debt,' *Journal of Political Economy*, vol. 87, no. 5, Part 1 (October 1979), pp 940–71. The basic idea is that the government should set tax rates so that it does not distort intertemporal decisions. If government tax policy is not intertemporally neutral, it distorts the otherwise (assumed) optimal decisions of the private sector. Also, frequent changes in tax rates can add disproportionately to the cost of revenue collection. The analysis cited above depends crucially on the assumption that private saving rises to offset government dissaving because individuals prepare for future increased taxes that would have to be imposed to service the debt. As a result of this assumption, deficits have no crowding out effect and no cyclical effect. Thus governments can focus their deficit policy solely on smoothing tax rates.
25. It should be noted that current fiscal policy, if it continues, will rapidly grow more expansionary over the course of the 1980s. CBO projects that the standardised budget deficit (inclusive of off-budget spending) will rise from 3.2 per cent of standardised GNP in 1984 to about 5 per cent in 1990. Thus, to maintain the same degree of fiscal stimulus as in 1984, the deficit would have to be smaller by $42 billion in 1985 and by $99 billion in 1990 than what CBO projects.

3 Britain's Budget Deficit in 1967–84: Its Consequences, Causes and Policies to Control it

Walter Eltis

In the period in question, Britain's Public Sector Borrowing Requirement has varied from negative borrowing, in 1969 and 1970, to $9\frac{1}{2}$ per cent of the gross national product in 1975. It was reduced from $4\frac{1}{2}$ per cent of the national product to zero by Mr Roy Jenkins, a Labour Chancellor of the Exchequer, allowed to rise to $7\frac{1}{2}$ per cent by Mr Edward Heath's Conservative government in 1970–73 and by a further 2 percentage points to $9\frac{1}{2}$ per cent in 1974–75 by Mr Harold Wilson's Labour government which succeeded it. The Labour party continued to govern from 1975 to 1979, but after 1976 led by Mr James Callaghan it ceased to favour high deficit policies and managed to reduce the deficit to an average of 5.1 per cent of the gross national product in 1977–79. Mrs Margaret Thatcher's Conservative government managed to reduce it further to an average of 3.2 per cent of the gross national product in 1981–84, and it hopes to reduce it to 1.75 per cent by 1989. In Britain, therefore, Conservative and Labour governments have each expanded the deficit sharply, and at other times both have also made strenuous efforts to reduce it. Since reducing the deficit involves either tax increases or public expenditure cuts (in the absence of phenomenal growth of a kind which Britain has not achieved), and these are both unpopular with electorates, it follows that both the British governing parties have at various times considered high deficits extremely damaging to the economy, so that it was worthwhile to eliminate them despite the high immediate political costs of doing so. It will be an object of this paper to say something about the adverse effects from high deficits which were perceived at the time, and which appeared to justify drastic policies for their reduction and indeed elimination.

TABLE 3.1 *Britain's public sector borrowing requirement as a percentage of GNP*

	Borrowing by			*Total borrowing*
	Central govt	*Local govt*	*Public corps*	
1967	−1.01	2.75	2.78	4.52
1968	−2.14	2.57	2.41	2.83
1969	−4.96	2.39	1.45	−1.13
1970	−4.38	2.38	1.90	−0.10
1971	−2.13	2.35	2.04	2.26
1972	−0.63	2.15	1.50	3.02
1973	0.65	3.17	1.63	5.45
1974	1.87	3.90	1.75	7.52
1975	4.51	2.60	2.39	9.50
1976	3.67	1.25	2.06	6.90
1977	1.74	0.98	1.04	3.76
1978	3.57	0.64	0.80	5.02
1979	3.30	1.20	1.91	6.41
1980	2.71	1.28	1.16	5.14
1981	3.96	0.10	0.09	4.16
1982	1.47	0.29	0.60	1.78
1983	3.04	0.41	0.39	3.83
1984	2.14	0.71	0.30	3.16

Note: The table shows public sector borrowing as a ratio of the gross national product at market prices. These statistics are published in the London Central Statistical Office's *National Income and Expenditure* and *Economic Trends*.

The actual data on Britain's Public Sector Borrowing Requirement is set out in Table 3.1. This shows the broad fluctuations which have been described.

The table divides borrowing into that by Central Government, Local Government and the Public Corporations, mainly the nationalised industries, and it shows that borrowing by Central Government has now become the dominant element in public sector borrowing. Until 1975, Local Government and the Public Corporations were responsible for most borrowing, and Central Government often ran substantial surpluses. As the central government guarantees the interest on all borrowing, attention will be focused on aggregate public sector borrowing from now on.

The table differs from official targets by showing public sector borrowing for each calendar year. The official targets for the Public Sector Borrowing Requirement are for financial years which run from April to April in the United Kingdom. Calendar years are far easier to find statistics for of the many kinds which will be shown alongside borrowing in the tables below, and there should be little difference whether public sector borrowing is measured from January to January, as in Table 3.1, or from April to April as in the government's targetry. There is strangely an important recent example where there is a large difference. Table 3.1 shows borrowing ratios of 4.16 per cent, 1.78 per cent and 3.83 per cent in 1981, 1982, and 1983 which points to a considerable relaxation of Mrs Margaret Thatcher's government's policies to reduce public sector borrowing during 1983, the year in which her government was re-elected with a greatly increased majority. The statistics for financial years show public sector borrowing of 3.5 per cent in 1982–83, and 3.2 per cent in 1983–84. This seeming steadiness of public sector borrowing hides the remarkable Keynesian fillip that the government slipped into the economy in the months before the 1983 general election which comes out clearly in Table 3.1.

An important objection to high and continuing government borrowing is that this will lead to a growing national debt, and to rising interest payments which the government must finance. If debt interest keeps rising in relation to the national income, then governments will need to borrow growing sums merely to keep pace with this interest. Such borrowing to finance debt interest makes possible neither increases in social expenditure by the government, nor reductions in rates of taxation to increase economic incentives. Hence, if the government has to borrow increasing sums to finance debt interest this will in time absorb all of its potential to borrow (which will necessarily have an upper limit) with the result that borrowing will come to fulfil no social purpose of any kind. At some further point in the future, if debt interest continues to mount the maximum the government can borrow will not suffice to finance even this, with the result that it can no longer honour its debts. This is happening today to many third world and Latin American countries which have involved themselves through excessive borrowing in annual interest bills which exceed their capacity to borrow. Defaults have been frequent in the past in Latin America and a new wave may be all but imminent.

Britain has been borrowing during almost every year since 1967, and often quite substantial fractions of the national income. Borrowing averaged 3.94 per cent of the national income in the eighteen years from 1967 to 1984, and the long-term interest rates at which the

British government borrowed rose from an average of 6.8 per cent in 1967 to 12.88 per cent in 1982, so a superficial observer would anticipate that there must have been a large increase in the ratio of debt interest to the British gross national product. In fact in 1967 the net debt interest of general government totalled £948 millions which amounted to 2.34 per cent of the gross national product. In 1982 it totalled £10,631 which amounted to just 3.29 per cent of the gross national product. Thus despite the near to doubling of interest rates and continuous borrowing, debt interest rose by less than 1 per cent of the national income. Why did this occur when, with doubled interest rates it would have doubled as a share of the national income, even if debt as a share of the national income was unchanged?

The answer lies in the fact that the national debt has fallen, despite all this borrowing, when it is measured in real terms, that is, when its total amount is corrected for inflation. 1975, the year in which the government borrowed 9.50 per cent of the gross national product may be taken as an example. In that year the government had total monetary liabilities of £52.9 billion, that is a net debt with a current monetary value of £52.9 billion. The gross national product in 1975 was £106.9 billion, so the monetary value of total debt amounted to 52.9/106.9 = 49.5 per cent of the gross national product. Starting with this debt of 49.5 per cent of the national income, the government then borrowed a further 9.5 per cent of the national income, but this did not raise the ratio of debt to the national income to 49.5 +9.5 = 59 per cent, because there was also inflation. Prices rose during 1975 by a record 23.6 per cent, and this eroded the government's net monetary liabilities or debt expressed in money values by a factor of 23.6/123.6 = 19.1 per cent. Thus inflation of 23.6 per cent reduced the real value of debt previously incurred by 19.1 per cent of that debt, and since this debt amounted to 49.5 per cent of the 1975 national income, the government made a capital gain as a result of inflation of 19.1/100 times 49.5 per cent = 9.45 per cent of the national income. As newly incurred debt amounted to 9.50 per cent of the national income the fall in the real value of previously incurred debt of 9.45 per cent of the national income almost entirely cancelled this out, so that the government owed virtually no more at the end of 1975 than it had owed at the beginning. The Bank of England publishes data regularly which show the effects of inflation on the real debt of the various sectors of the British economy, and this shows that the real value of the net monetary liabilities of the public sector

TABLE 3.2 *The real borrowing of the British government as a percentage of GNP*

	Public Sector Borrowing Requirement	*Effect of inflation on real value of debt*	*Real net borrowing*
1967	4.5	−2.0	2.5
1968	2.8	−5.2	2.4
1969	−1.1	−4.0	−5.1
1970	−0.1	−5.2	−5.3
1971	2.3	−5.5	−3.2
1972	3.0	−4.8	−1.8
1973	5.5	−5.4	0.1
1974	7.5	−10.9	−3.4
1975	9.5	−11.2	−1.7
1976	6.9	−5.9	1.0
1977	3.8	−6.5	−2.7
1978	5.0	−4.0	1.0
1979	6.4	−7.6	−1.2
1980	5.1	−5.8	−0.7
1981	4.2	−4.9	−0.7
1982	1.8	−2.6	−0.8
1983	3.8	−2.0	1.8
1984	3.2	−2.5	0.7

Note: The effect of inflation on the real value of debt is taken from the *Bank of England Quarterly Bulletin* (June 1984), p. 231, for the years 1970–83, and from C. T. Taylor & A. R. Threadgold, "'Real' national saving and its sectoral composition", *Bank of England Discussion Paper*, no. 6 (October 1979), for the years 1967–69. 1984 is estimated using the same procedure.

has been falling in most years since 1967. The government's real debt has therefore been falling almost without interruption, despite the continuous borrowing set out in Table 3.1. The Bank of England's estimations, which correspond almost precisely to those arrived at by the simple method set out above, are shown in Table 3.2, which demonstrates how, in almost every year since 1967, the capital gain resulting from inflation which the government has enjoyed (through the tendency of inflation to reduce the real value of its monetary liabilities) has exceeded new borrowing by the government, with the result that there has been a continual falling tendency in the real debt of the British government.

It will be evident from the table that the real indebtedness of the British government fell by approximately 20 per cent of the national income from 1967 to 1984. As the real national income rose 40 per

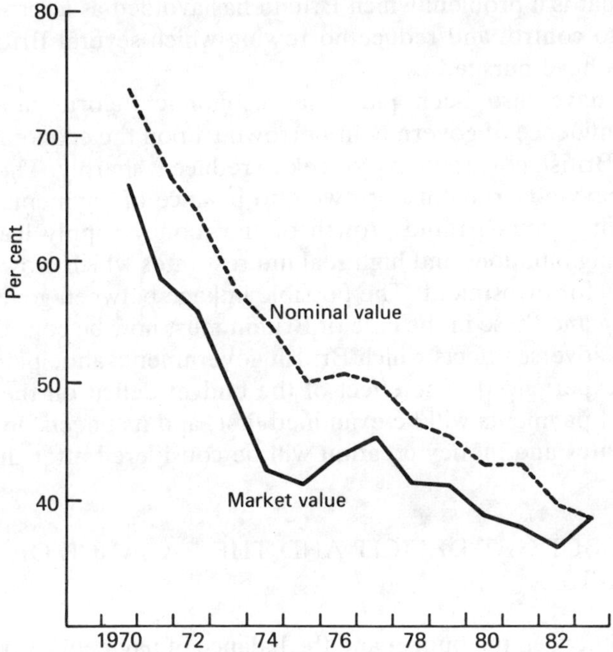

SOURCE: *Bank of England Quarterly Bulletin* (June 1984, p. 233).

FIGURE 3.1 *Public sector net monetary liabilities as a proportion of GDP*

cent in this period, government debt as a fraction of the national income fell by more than 20 per cent, indeed by as much as 42 per cent. The almost continuous fall of public sector debt as a ratio of the national income is illustrated in Figure 3.1.

The explanation of why the interest cost of British government debt rose only from 2.34 to 3.29 per cent of the national income, from 1967 to 1984, despite a near-doubling of interest rates, is therefore that debt has fallen sharply as a ratio of the national income.

Given the large fall in debt in relation to the national income, why have various British governments been so concerned to reduce public sector borrowing, often at considerable political cost? One explanation is of course that if strenuous efforts had not been made to reduce public sector borrowing in 1967–70, in 1976–78 and in 1979–84, debt might have risen sharply in relation to the national income, even in real terms, as it has done in so many countries in the 1970s and the

1980s. That is a problem which Britain has avoided as a result of the policies to control and reduce borrowing which several British governments have pursued.

There have also been particular economic theories about the adverse influence of government borrowing upon the economy which have led British governments to seek to reduce it sharply. These have linked heavy government borrowing to balance of payments deficits on current account, rapid growth of the money supply leading to accelerating inflation, and high real interest rates which crowded out private sector investment. The possible linkage between government borrowing and these in the case of Britain must now be considered to see if the adverse effects which British governments anticipated were actually experienced. The effect of the budget deficit on the British balance of payments will be examined first, and its effects on saving, interest rates and money creation will be considered after this.

3.1 THE BUDGET DEFICIT AND THE BALANCE OF PAYMENTS

The link between the budget and the balance of payments is best seen via the well known accounting identity that:

$$\begin{matrix}\text{Private}\\ \text{Investment}\end{matrix} + \begin{matrix}\text{Government}\\ \text{expenditure}\end{matrix} + \text{Exports} \equiv \begin{matrix}\text{Private}\\ \text{saving}\end{matrix} + \text{Taxation} + \text{Imports}$$

The left hand side of this expression includes the injections into a country's income flows and the right hand side, the leakages, and aggregate injections must equal aggregate leakages. This expression can be rearranged as follows:

$$\left(\begin{matrix}\text{Government}\\ \text{expenditure}\end{matrix} - \text{Taxation}\right) \equiv (\text{Imports} - \text{Exports}) +$$

$$\left(\begin{matrix}\text{Private}\\ \text{saving}\end{matrix} - \begin{matrix}\text{Private}\\ \text{Investment}\end{matrix}\right)$$

That is, the budget deficit, viz the excess of government expenditure over taxation, must be identically equal to the balance of payments deficit on current account, viz the excess of imports over exports, plus the excess of private saving over private investment. One way of interpreting this expression is that it indicates that a budget deficit must be financed either from overseas via the capital account of the balance of payments, which will provide a capital inflow that will match any excess of imports over exports, or at home via an excess of private saving over private investment. It follows that if there is a large budget deficit, there must either be a large excess of private saving over investment, or else a considerable excess of imports over exports, that is, a current account deficit that is the inevitable counterpart of any financing of the budget deficit from overseas.

In Britain in the 1960s and the early 1970s it was widely believed that the excess of private saving over private investment would tend to be fairly stable, and this excess can be described as the financial surplus of the private sector. The excess of private saving over investment allows the private sector to acquire financial assets or to repay debts, so it is in financial surplus. If the excess of private saving over private investment is stable, then a large increase in the budget deficit must be matched by an adverse change of similar size in the balance of payments on current account. If the budget deficit grows sharply, debt will only be financeable at home if private saving rises relative to investment. If it does not, then the increase in the budget deficit will have to be financed from overseas which will involve an increase in imports relative to exports. Similarly, if the budget deficit is eliminated as in 1969 and 1970 while the excess of saving over investment remains stable, then the counterpart to the improvement in the budget will be an equivalent strengthening of the balance of payments.

Figure 3.2 illustrates the application of these propositions. Where the public sector is in deficit, it has a negative financial surplus or rate of acquisition of financial assets, and the public sector line shows a negative rate of acquisition of financial assets of between 3 and 5 per cent of the gross national product from 1961 to 1968. In these years it is acquiring financial assets negatively because it is selling debt amounting to 3 to 5 per cent of the gross national product each year. The personal sector is at the same time showing a financial surplus of between 2 and 3 per cent of the gross national product, that is it is saving more than it is investing with the result that it can acquire financial assets amounting to this fraction of the national product. But what if, as in 1967, the public sector has a financial deficit of almost 5 per cent of the national income, so that it sells assets equivalent to 5 per cent of the national income, while the personal sector buys assets equivalent to only $2\frac{1}{2}$ per cent. The remaining $2\frac{1}{2}$ per cent must be bought either by the company sector or the overseas sector, that is by foreigners. If, as in Figure 3.2, the

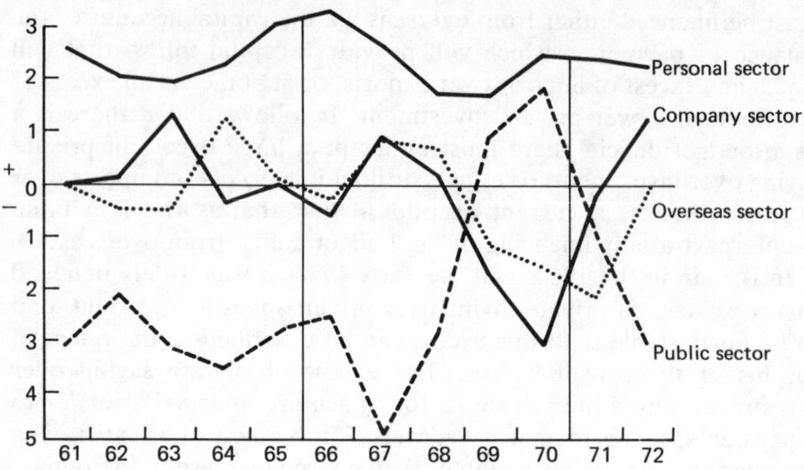

SOURCE: *The National Institute Economic Review* (May 1973).

FIGURE 3.2 *Net acquisition of financial assets as a percentage of GNP*

overseas sector buys some of the these excess government assets that the personal sector cannot buy, then foreigners are on balance acquiring British shares, and the current account of the balance of payments is in deficit as it was in 1967 when sterling was devalued from \$2.80 to \$2.40. The diagram shows that where the budget moves into surplus in 1969–70, the personal sector continues to buy shares equivalent to $2\frac{1}{2}$ per cent of the national product, but the government is no longer selling shares. The personal sector is therefore buying shares from the overseas sector (and of course companies). In so far as it buys shares from the overseas sector, Britain is acquiring shares from foreigners, so the capital account of the balance of payments is in deficit, and the current account is in surplus. The diagram shows how, when the budget swings into larger deficit, that is, when the government sells more financial assets, then at the same time the overseas sector moves into surplus, that is foreigners buy some of those assets, so the capital account of the balance of payments necessarily moves into surplus, and the current account into deficit.

The net acquisition of financial assets of all the sectors must sum to zero because financial assets cannot be acquired by some without equivalent debts accruing at the same time to others. The evidence of the diagram made many in Britain believe at this time that this zero sum rule genuinely meant that if British governments significantly increased the rate at which they acquired debts then, because of the stability of the personal sector, the rate at which foreigners acquired British assets would rise correspondingly. The National Institute of Economic and Social Research inferred from the data in the diagram that a £1 change in net acquisitions by the public sector tends to be associated with a £0.4 change in the overseas sector and a £0.6 change in the company sector in the opposite direction. That is, a cut in the budget deficit of £1 billion would tend to improve the balance of payments by £400 million, and at the same time reduce company savings relative to investment by £600 million. Thus tightening the budget would damage the finances of companies by 60 per cent of the budgetary squeeze, but improve the balance of payments by 40 per cent of the improvement in the budget.

Lord Kaldor, then an economic adviser to the Treasury, perceived these regularities during the 1960s and it may well have been advice based on them which led Mr Jenkins to actually move the budget into surplus in 1969. Britain's overwhelming problem in 1967–70 was believed to be the balance of payments. The pound was devalued from $2.80 to $2.40 in 1967 in the hope that the balance of payments constraint on growth would thereby be removed and it was essential to exploit that devaluation successfully. Lord Kaldor and Mr Jenkins believed that exploiting the devaluation and turning round the balance of payments would involve a massive budgetary swing from deficit into surplus, and this was indeed achieved. The current account of the balance of payments moved at the same time from deficits of £269 million in 1967 and £244 million in 1968 to surpluses of £505 million in 1969 and £823 million in 1970.

During the 1970 general election campaign, Lord Kaldor was concerned that the Labour government, which he had persuaded to balance the budget, might lose power, and that a successor Conservative government might, as it did, re-open the budget deficit, and he wrote to *The Times* on 8 June 1970, just before the election, to say that if the public sector ever again became a net borrower instead of a net repayer of debt, then 'as sure as night follows day, our balance of payments difficulties would reappear again'.

The relationship he predicted continued to hold until 1974, and while the Public Sector Borrowing Requirement rose from zero in 1970 to 5.5 per cent of the gross national product in 1973 and 7.5 per

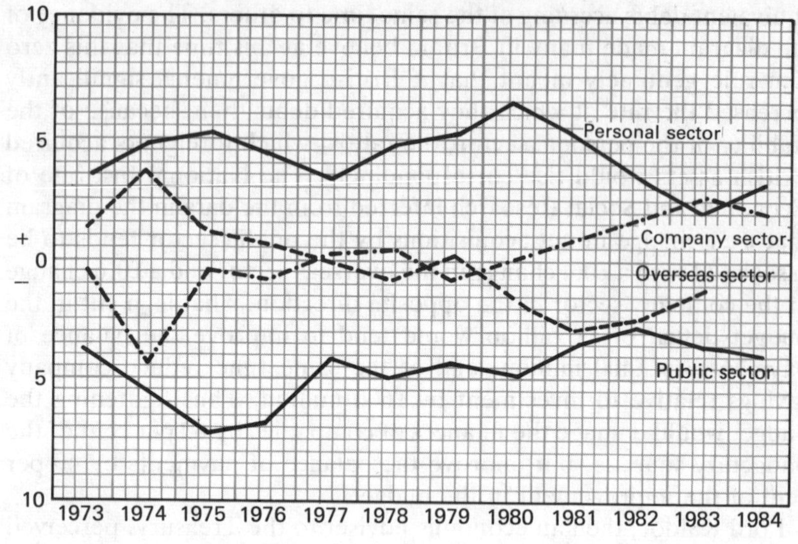

SOURCE: *Economic Trends*.

FIGURE 3.3 *Net Acquisition of financial assets as a percentage of GNP*

cent of the gross national product in 1974, the current account swung from a surplus of 1.6 per cent of the gross national product in 1970 to deficits of 1.3 per cent of the gross national product in 1973 and 3.9 per cent in 1974.

But a test of a hypothesis is its continuing power to predict, and the extension of the National Institute's table to the next decade, 1974–84, does not repeat the elegant pattern of the original graph (see Figure 3.3). The net acquisition of financial assets of the personal sector is no longer the steady 2 to 3 per cent of the gross national product of the period 1962–72: it actually reaches $6\frac{1}{2}$ per cent in 1980. But the main change between the two diagrams is in the interrelationship between the balance of payments and the company sector. From 1962 to 1972 the financial surpluses of the company sector and the overseas sector tended to deteriorate and improve together, and these movements in both were associated with movements in the budget. Thus where the budget moved into larger deficit so that the acquisition of debts by the public sector increased, both the company sector's and the overseas sector's finances improved.

The strengthening of the overseas sector meant that the balance of payments moved into deficit because it was the finances of foreigners that were being reinforced, and the larger surpluses of the company sector meant that retained profits were rising faster than investment. Thus deficit financing damaged the balance of payments and at the same time improved company finances.

The simple relationship that a superficial observer would notice in the 1973–84 diagram is that the financial surpluses of the company sector and the overseas sectors now move in opposite directions: they are virtually mirror images. Thus, as the finances of British companies strengthen, those of the overseas sector, that is those of foreigners, weaken, so the balance of payments improves at the same time as the finances of British companies. It does not require sophisticated econometrics to indicate that North Sea oil simultaneously improves both. There is also some kind of connection between the financial deficit of the public sector and the surplus of the overseas sector, but it is far weaker than in 1962–72. The advocates of the orthodoxy stated above, that the budget and the balance of payments were mirror images, became very quiet when the budget deficit rose from 7.5 to 9.5 per cent of the gross national product between 1974 and 1975, and the current account deficit of the balance of payments, instead of rising further, actually fell from 3.9 to 1.4 per cent of the national product. In general terms the current account improved at the same time as tighter budgetary policies were followed in most of the next eight years, but no one spoke any longer of a predictable and mechanical link of the kind that Lord Kaldor originally perceived.

Because the financial surpluses of the public sector, the personal sector, the company sector and the overseas sector must sum to zero, there must be interactions between large changes in any one of these and the other three. But in the absence of simple rules affecting one of them (such as that the financial surplus of the personal sector is always 2 to 3 per cent of the gross national product) nothing exact can be said about how the other three will react when the financial surplus of the public sector rises or falls. It may be that the surplus of the company or of the personal sector will rise when the deficit of the public sector rises, as in 1975, in which case there will be no adverse balance of payments effects, or it may be that a larger public deficit will not be matched by larger domestic surpluses elsewhere in which case the balance of payments will deteriorate.

It is however a rule of arithmetic, as Lord Kaldor perceived, that a deterioration in the finances of the public sector must be matched either by equivalent balance of payments deterioration, or else by an equivalent increase in surpluses in either the personal sector or the company sector. Thus, if the budget is allowed to deteriorate when there is no reason to believe that the personal or the company sector will raise its saving more than its investment, there must be serious deterioration in the balance of payments. That is a truth which many countries with budget deficits substantially larger than Britain's (such as the United States in the 1980s) have ignored, and consequently have destroyed their balance of payments.

After 1975 when the link between the budget and the balance of payments ceased to appear a key one in Britain, attention switched to the link between the size of the budget deficit and the rate of growth of the money supply, which was increasingly seen as an important element in the explanation of inflation. With inflation at 23.6 per cent in 1975, this was widely believed to be Britain's major problem in the next years. Mr Callaghan's Labour government sought to reduce it to around 10 per cent, and Mrs Thatcher's Conservative government which took office in 1979 actually hopes to reduce inflation to less than 4 per cent. Control of the rate of growth of the money supply, which is believed to require a declining budget deficit as monetary growth rates are reduced, has thus become a central element in macroeconomic policy in Britain.

The interconnection between the budget deficit and the rate of growth of the money supply became an important influence on economic policy with regard to the budget in 1976, and it became *the* consideration on which budgetary policy focused upon Mrs Margaret Thatcher's election in 1979. Some of the evidence relating to the connection between the budget deficit and the rate of growth of the money supply in Britain must therefore be presented.

3.2 THE PUBLIC SECTOR BORROWING REQUIREMENT AND THE RATE OF MONETARY GROWTH

It is well-known that a budget deficit must be financed either by borrowing or through the monetisation of debt. All government expenditures involve cheques written by the government which will be credited to some bank account or other. Taxation involves the writing of cheques to the government's account in the Central Bank, and the running down of accounts in the commercial banks. If the government spends £100 billion and taxes £90 billion, it writes cheques for £100 billion and receives cheques for £90 billion, so the cash reserves of the commercial banks will be boosted by £10 billion. This infusion of high-powered-money to the commercial banks encourages them to increase their lending by a multiple of £10 billion. But the £10 billion will be removed from their accounts if the government sells bonds or bills for £10 billion to finance the deficit, because this will involve the writing of a further £10 billion of cheques to the Central Bank. So the budget deficit will have no tendency to lead to faster rates of money creation in so far as it is financed by borrowing from the private sector, and it will have a very considerable effect on the rate of growth of the money supply in so far as the government fails to sell bills or bonds to finance it.

The general view is that governments also have interest rate targets which limit the bills and bonds they can dispose of. They could sell an almost unlimited quantity of bills and bonds if they were indifferent to their price, so they could always finance their deficits through borrowing if they were willing to allow interest rates to rise to whatever rate had to be offered to dispose of the necessary shares. But because high interest rates are unappealing to governments, only a limited quantity of shares can be disposed of at the government's target interest rates which may be artificially low, with the result that part of a large deficit will tend to be financed through the banking system and therefore monetised. Has this happened significantly in Britain? The evidence on the size of the budget deficit and the rate of monetary growth since 1970 is presented in Table 3.3.

The table places the rates of monetary growth in the following twelve months against the Public Sector Borrowing Requirement of each year, and three rates of monetary growth, those in M1, £M3 and PSL2 are shown. M1 is cash plus current account bank deposits, £M3 also includes deposits which are held in savings accounts on which interest is earned, while PSL2 (where PSL stands for Private Sector Liquidity) also includes deposits in building societies which can be withdrawn, like bank deposits, almost at will. The three rates of monetary growth differ for a variety of institutional reasons, but British governments have recently been careful to look at all three measures of the money supply (and others in addition now, i.e., M0 and M2) when assessing the nature and effectiveness of monetary pressures on the real economy.

In the table these three rates of monetary growth are contrasted with the rate of growth of the nominal gross national product, because a monetary explosion which then adds to inflation will show

TABLE 3.3 *Monetary growth and the Public Sector borrowing requirement*

		Annual percentage growth in the next twelve months			
	PSBR (%)	*Nominal GNP*	*MI*	*£M3*	*PSL2*
1970	−0.1	12.1	11.0	11.0	10.8
1971	2.3	10.7	13.4	21.7	19.1
1972	3.0	16.3	12.4	23.0	18.6
1973	5.5	13.8	0.2	18.0	13.4
1974	7.5	25.1	15.3	9.2	10.0
1975	9.5	19.7	15.3	8.2	15.3
1976	6.9	13.3	10.9	7.6	8.3
1977	3.8	15.7	22.1	15.6	15.0
1978	5.0	17.1	12.3	12.7	14.8
1979	6.4	16.3	6.6	15.8	12.5
1980	5.1	10.8	10.0	16.6	13.6
1981	4.2	9.1	8.0	14.8	9.6
1982	1.8	9.1	14.3	11.1	12.3
1983	3.8	6.9	13.7	9.9	13.9
1984	3.2	8.9	18.4	13.8	13.3

SOURCE: *Economic Trends*.

up first as a rate of growth of the money supply in excess of the rate of growth of the money national income. If the money supply merely grows at roughly the same rate as the national income, then no *extra* inflationary pressures are to be anticipated from monetary growth because this is merely keeping track with the transactions, etc., which will in any case now need to be financed. But a rate of monetary growth which substantially exceeds the rate of growth of the money national income will put extra upward pressures on a variety of markets which will tend to raise output and final goods and portfolio prices. Thus the monetisation of a large budget deficit would be likely to show up in faster growth of the money supply than in the nominal national income in the following twelve months.

There are in fact no instances where this occurred. Two measures of the money supply, £M3 and PSL2, grew far faster than the nominal national income in 1971–72 and in 1972–73, while all three grew faster in 1984/85, but 1971, 1972, and 1984 were all years in which the budget deficit was small. The excess monetary growth was due to institutional change in the British banking system, and many believe that the great acceleration in inflation in 1973–74 and in 1974–75 (which shows up here as very large growth rates in the nominal national income) was due to this previous monetary growth. Once the budget deficit became large in 1974, 1975 and 1976, monetary growth actually slowed down quite sharply, and inflation fell back in the following years. Thus the very large deficits were financed through borrowing, and not monetisation. Some of the measures of the money supply grew quite rapidly in relation to the rate of growth of the nominal national income in 1980, 1981, 1982 and 1983 and all grew rapidly in 1984–85, but these were again years in which the deficit was of modest size. The faster growth of the wider monetary aggregates can again be explained by institutional change in the banking system, as can the rapid growth of M1 in 1982–83 and 1983–84. More M1 deposits began to receive interest in those years, which persuaded the British authorities to begin to regard M1 as a poor indicator of the growth of transactions balances and to switch their attention to M0, the monetary base, which has been growing extremely slowly since 1980.

There is no evidence that British deficits have as yet been associated with acceleration in the rate of monetary expansion. It can therefore be concluded that they have been financed through the sale of whatever quantity of bonds and bills needed to be sold, so their main effect will have been on the price the government received for those bonds. Hence the main effect of the budget deficit will have been on the rate of interest which the British government had to pay, and therefore on other interest rates in Britain.

The possibility which must be considered next is therefore that government borrowing has tended to raise the rate of interest in Britain, which could then be expected to crowd out private sector expenditures on capital investment.

3.3 PUBLIC SECTOR BORROWING AND THE RATE OF INTEREST IN BRITAIN

It is well-known that the interest rates of particular countries depend on a variety of circumstances. They will be higher, for instance, if monetary conditions are tight rather than loose, if inflationary expectations are stronger, or if governments need to market more debt. At the same time the interest rates of all countries depend on the level of United States interest rates. World financial markets are very much linked and multinational companies and banks can move vast sums across the exchanges rapidly to take advantage of perceived interest rate differences between countries. It can be suggested in summary that all interest rates will be related to the interest rate of the United States. Countries perceived to hold currencies which are advantageous compared to the United States dollar will be able to pay lower interest rates than the United States. Countries with currencies that are judged to be weaker will have to pay more interest than the United States. Any country which seeks to market bills or bonds is adding to the world stock of bills or bonds, and apart from the United States it adds to this imperceptibly because the borrowing of most countries has an extremely slight effect on the total stock of bonds in the world.

But as each country sells bills or bonds, it may have a considerable effect on the stock of its own bonds or bills in the world. As this stock rises, so will the risk that is perceived to arise in holding bonds and bills in the currency of that country, so the interest differential it has to pay in relation to United States interest rates will also rise. A country which is reducing its stock of bonds in the world in relation to those of other countries will at the same time reduce the risk that is perceived to arise from holding assets in its currency, with its taxpayers obliged to provide future interest.

The main effect of British government borrowing should not therefore be on British interest rates as such. It is rather that British interest rates can be expected to rise in relation to United States interest rates where British borrowing rises, and fall in relation to United States rates as borrowing falls. That is in fact exactly what can be observed from the evidence of the post-1970 period which is set out in Table 3.4. Here the interest rates on government bonds with 20 years to maturity are set out for both countries, and it will be evident that the extra interest which the British government has to pay rises sharply from 2.1 per cent in 1970, when the British budget is balanced, to a peak of over 6 per cent from 1974 to 1976, when the British Public Sector Borrowing Requirement reaches 9.5 per cent of the gross national product. After this the extra interest which the British government has to pay falls continuously until in 1983 and 1984 the United States government actually has to pay more interest than the British government. In these years the United States national debt is actually rising sharply in relation to the American national product, while, as Figure 3.1 showed, British government debt is falling in real terms and still more in relation to the national income.

Table 3.4 shows how the alternative explanation of relative long-

TABLE 3.4 *Long-term interest rates in the United States and the United Kingdom*

	20 year govt bonds(%)			*Excess UK inflation in previous*		
	UK	*USA*	*UK–USA*	*5 years*	*2 years*	*1 year (%)*
1970	9.2	6.9	2.3	0.3	0.2	0.5
1971	8.9	6.1	2.8	1.1	2.7	5.0
1972	9.0	6.0	3.0	1.7	4.2	3.5
1973	10.8	7.1	3.7	2.1	2.7	1.9
1974	14.8	8.0	6.8	3.1	3.2	4.5
1975	14.4	8.2	6.2	5.2	8.2	13.8
1976	14.4	7.9	6.5	6.7	11.2	10.2
1977	12.7	7.7	5.0	7.7	9.5	8.8
1978	2.5	8.5	4.0	7.4	4.6	0.7
1979	13.0	10.0	3.0	6.8	1.3	2.1
1980	13.8	11.4	2.4	5.3	3.0	3.9
1981	14.7	13.7	1.0	4.8	2.6	1.4
1982	12.9	12.9	0	2.0	1.9	2.4
1983	10.8	11.3	–0.5	1.8	1.8	1.3
1984	10.7	11.7	–1.0	2.0	1.0	0.7
1985	10.4	10.8	–0.4	1.8	1.8	3.0

SOURCE: *Economic Trends, Statistical Abstract of the United States, Federal Reserve Bank Quarterly Bulletin* and *National Institute Economic Review.*

term interest rates, namely differences in rates of inflation between the two countries, is not nearly as sensitive as differences in borrowing in picking out the major turning points. Thus the interest differential widens from an excess United Kingdom rate of 3.0 percentage points to an excess of 6.8 percentage points from 1972 to 1974. The excess inflation of the United Kingdom hardly changes from 1972 to 1974, but the British Public Sector Borrowing Requirement rises from 3.0 per cent of the gross national product, which is well in line with previous trends in 1972, to an unprecedented 7.5 per cent in 1974. In 1974 United Kingdom interest rates are 6.8 percentage points above United States rates, but United Kingdom inflation is only 3 to $4\frac{1}{2}$ percentage points above United States inflation. The interest differential remains high in 1977 and 1978 by which time British inflation is seen to be higher than the United States' inflation by over 5 percentage points in the three previous years, but after 1978 the interest differential narrows sharply, to 3.0 percentage points in 1979, 2.4 in 1980, 1.0 in 1981, and United States interest rates actually exceed British rates in 1983, 1984 and 1985. Inflation comes

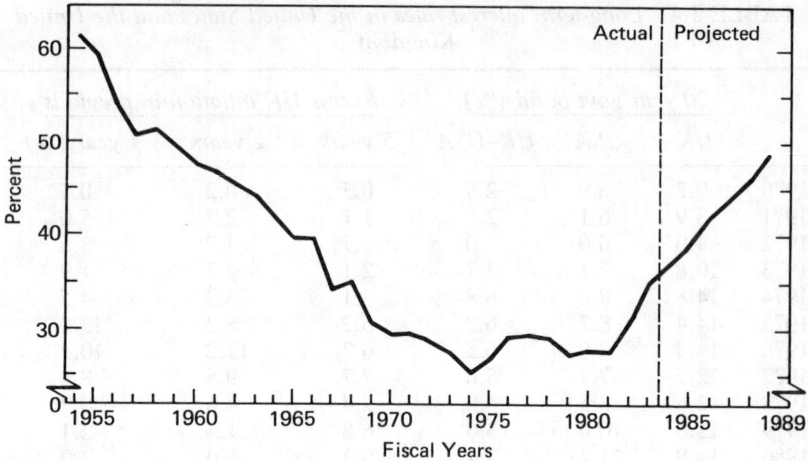

SOURCE: Congressional Budget Office.

FIGURE 3.4 *Debt held by the public (excluding federal reserve) as a percent of GNP, year end*

down sharply in both countries in the 1980s but British inflation remains persistently higher than United States inflation by at least 1 percentage point per annum. Why then does the British long-term interest rate fall gradually in relation to the United States rate? Portfolio theory points to an entirely straightforward answer. Figure 3.4 shows how sharply United States government debt rises relative to the United States gross national product after 1979, while Figure 3.1 above showed how sharply British government debt has been falling relative to the British gross national product. As the United States gross national product has been rising relative to the British national product, United States debt has been rising that much faster relative to British debt in international portfolios. As the United States debt that international portfolio holders have had to include in their portfolios has risen, the interest that the United States government has had to offer has risen relative to the interest the British government has had to offer to persuade banks and financial institutions to hold diminishing totals of real British government debt.

In the early 1970s the British interest differential was approximately in line with the inflation differential. In the middle 1980s it was perhaps 2 percentage points below the inflation differential: that is, in 1983, 1984 and 1985 British interest rates were below the long-term United States' rates while British inflation was still between 1 and 2 per cent per annum faster than the United States' inflation. This substantial shift in relative interest rates in favour of the United Kingdom could well be a reflection of the changes in the relative quantities of British and United States' government bonds – which the diagrams show, and which are a consequence of persistent British policies to reduce government borrowing so that this has been negative in real terms for some time – and strong United States' policies to raise government borrowing in both nominal and real terms. Markets have then predicted that future inflation rates will rise and future exchange rates fall, where a country's borrowing is such that the ratio of its bonds in world portfolios has to rise. Portfolio holders dislike raising the debt of any one government that they hold, because that country's borrowing may be monetised in future, and this would raise inflation and produce exchange depreciation. Alternatively that country may have to raise its interest rates in future as the ratio of its debt in world portfolios rises, which would tend to raise its interest rate relative to those of other countries in the short term also.

Certainly the evidence is compatible with the view that British interest rates were strongly influenced by the Public Sector Borrowing Requirement. They rose in relation to United States rates while the Public Sector Borrowing Requirement increased from zero in 1970 to 9.5 per cent of the gross national product in 1975. British interest rates then fell relative to United States rates – as British borrowing was cut back to 3 to 4 per cent of the gross national product, while United States government borrowing rose to 7 per cent of the gross national product in 1983 and 5 per cent in 1984 and 1985.

If borrowing influences the interest rate in this way, how will it influence private sector investment through the well-known crowding-out mechanisms?

3.4 HAS THERE BEEN 'CROWDING OUT' IN BRITAIN?

If public sector borrowing influences interest rates, it will also influence private sector investment in so far as this is sensitive to the rate of interest. According to Keynesian theory, crowding out should only occur where an economy is working close to its capacity limits. But the argument of the previous section has suggested that high government borrowing will influence the rate of interest at all times and not merely at cyclical peaks. This is because international portfolio holders will not look at the unemployment statistics of a country when deciding the terms on which they will add shares issued by its government to their portfolios. They will be concerned instead by the quantity they already hold, and whether their exposure to the shares of that country and government is becoming unduly high. If the risk attached to that currency is perceived to rise, extra interest will need to be offered to dispose of the necessary shares, whatever the level of domestic employment.

It is because all the shares that are issued have to be absorbed into portfolios that it is actual and not full employment corrected deficits that matter in the determination of interest rates. It is well-known that public sector deficits deteriorate in recession because tax revenues fall and government expenditure rises, since government finance is needed for the support of the unemployed and for nationalised companies which earn smaller profits or make losses when demand is weak. Many economists have demonstrated that if a budget is adjusted to what it would be at full employment, current deficits will be much smaller (assuming the extra revenues that would be earned at full employment but which the government is not actually receiving) or there may even be surpluses. The crucial weakness in these corrections is that if there is an actual budget deficit while the economy is in recession, government bonds and bills will need to be marketed to finance *all* of it. That is the vital consideration. There is the added weakness in the so-called full employment corrected deficits that those who estimate them often assume that economies will return to a wholly unrealistic future level of employment so that they assume revenues which may not be earned for decades on a balance of probabilities.

There is however one important sense in which the Keynesian idea that deficits only affect investment adversely when the economy is close to its capacity limits is correct. Deficits will tend to make interest rates higher than they otherwise would have been at all times, but it is only when the economy is close to full capacity working that they will affect investment adversely. This is because they will tend to raise effective demand in the short term through the direct and indirect effects of higher government expenditure or lower taxation upon the markets of domestic producers. As deficits will make demand higher in the short term than it otherwise would have been, supply and output will be higher provided that an economy is not close to its capacity limits, and one of the indirect effects of more buoyant demand conditions and of higher levels of output is a higher level of capital investment. Thus even though interest rates will be higher than they otherwise would have been, investment will be higher in so far as better sales have a stronger positive effect on investment than the negative effect of the higher rate of interest. It is widely believed that this is the case, so, as an economy expands towards full-capacity working assisted by deficit-financed spending, investment will in all probability be higher than it otherwise would have been. It is only at full capacity working that there is no room for extra government consumption and investment, and extra private investment in addition. The possible adverse effects of high government deficits upon capital spending can therefore only be assessed when an economy is judged to be close to its capacity limits. Britain may have been in this situation in 1970, in 1973 and in 1979, and in Table 3.5 some of the statistics for these three years are compared.

The excess of private sector saving over investment should equal public sector borrowing plus the current account balance of payments surplus, according to the formula on page 82, and it will be evident from the table that the discrepancy in each of these years is less than 1 per cent of the gross national product, so the table has managed to capture the orders of magnitude of the broad flows. In current money values, the private sector had a surplus of saving over investment of 1.2 per cent of the gross national product in 1970, 3.4 per cent in 1973 and 4.0 per cent in 1979. In 1973 the government also ran a surplus of 1.3 per cent of the gross national product; that is, on balance it was buying shares rather than selling, which together with the private sector's excess of saving over investment could have produced a current account trade surplus of 2.5 per cent of the gross national product: the actual surplus is 1.6 per cent. In 1973 the surplus of private saving over investment is 3.4 per cent of the gross national product, but the government is selling shares to the extent of 3.7 per cent of the gross national product, which produces a predicted current account deficit of 0.3 per cent of the gross national product: the actual deficit is 1.3 per cent. In 1979 the private sector surplus of saving is 4.0 per cent of the gross national product, the government actually borrows 4.6 per cent, and the current account deficit is 0.3 per cent against the predicted 0.6 per cent. The heavier government borrowing in 1979 and 1973 than in 1970 is not associated with less private or company investment, for these are higher fractions of the national income in 1979 and 1973 than in 1970. The deterioration in

TABLE 3.5 *Sectoral saving and government borrowing in Britain (% of GNP)*

	Private saving		*Private investment*		*Surplus of private saving*	*Actual public borrowing*	*Trade surplus*
	Personal	*Company*	*Personal*	*Company*			
1970	6.1	6.2	2.5	8.6	1.2	–1.3	1.6
1973	7.8	9.7	4.1	10.0	3.4	3.7	–1.3
1972	9.4	8.9	4.3	10.0	4.0	4.6	–0.3
	Inflation adjusted using Bank of England's method						
1970	0.7	7.0	2.5	8.6	–3.4	–4.0	1.6
1973	1.7	10.8	4.1	10.0	–2.6	–1.6	–1.3
1979	1.6	9.9	4.3	10.0	–2.8	–2.9	–0.3

Note: Saving and investment are expressed net of stock appreciation; actual public borrowing is the 'net total financial transactions' of the public sector which differs from the 'Public Sector Borrowing Requirement' mainly because of differences between required borrowing and actual accruals.

SOURCE: The Bank of England adjustments are from *BEQB* (June 1984), p. 231.

the budget is associated with deficits in the balance of payments when in 1970 there was a current account surplus, but there is no ascertainable adverse effect on investment, though it stands to reason that the higher interest rates in 1973 (3.7 percentage points above United States levels, against 2.3 per cent above in 1970 and 3.0 per cent above in 1979) must have had some tendency to make investment in 1973 and 1974 lower than it would have been in the absence of the high borrowing that produced these exceptional relative interest rates.

The inflation adjusted statistics show far lower personal saving, because the capital losses that the personal sector suffers as a result of inflation are deducted, while the capital gains that the government makes are added in, as in Table 3.2. With these adjusted figures, private investment exceeds private saving by about 3 per cent of the gross national product in each year. The government in real terms runs a surplus, because the real national debt is falling. This real government surplus is as high as 4 per cent of the gross national product in 1970 when the balance of payments current account is in surplus, but it is far smaller in 1973 and 1979, when the balance of payments current account is in deficit. With the inflation adjusted figures there is no reason to suppose that there is any crowding out at all, because the government is a net lender to the private sector and not a net borrower. The general stability of the inflation adjusted data with fairly stable private sector personal saving, and private surpluses of investment over saving, and indeed stable real government surpluses, may well be a factor which lies behind the stability of private sector investment as a ratio of the gross national product.

If the inflation adjusted data shows that the government was at no point borrowing in real terms, why then did British interest rates rise to 6 or 7 per cent above United States levels in 1974, 1975 and 1976? It may well be that international portfolio holders who have such influence on these pay more regard to nominal borrowing, which was very high in this period, than to real borrowing, which was negative. In so far as this is the case, governments must also pursue policies which control nominal borrowing. The fact that debt is being written down by inflation is not an attraction to foreign portfolio holders, and they may in any case be seriously frightened of the future prospects of actually receiving interest on the government debt of a country which is borrowing heavily in nominal terms.

It is reassuring however that there is no hard evidence in Britain's case that the heavy nominal borrowing of the 1970s was associated with a squeeze on private sector investment.

3.5 CONCLUSION: THE RATIONALE FOR CURRENT FISCAL POLICY IN BRITAIN

It will be evident that British governments have succeeded in steadily reducing the national debt in relation to the national income, and in avoiding serious adverse pressures from the budget upon the balance of payments or the rate of growth of the money supply. Governments have also succeeded in reducing British interest rates by several percentage points in relation to the United States rates, so that British rates have been below the United States rates in 1983 and 1984 and approximately equal to them in 1985. What was the thinking in 1985 behind these policies, and what are the implications for the British budget deficit if present policies continue to be pursued?

The government's main objective has been to create a stable and predictable financial environment within which private sector companies can take investment and employment decisions. These private companies are deemed to determine the pace at which employment and output will grow in Britain and the government is determined to create an environment where they will be able to borrow at low interest rates, and expand without competing pressures on financial markets from government borrowing. The objective has therefore been to achieve neutral pressures from the government deficit.

At the same time it has been an objective to bring inflation down steadily by reducing the rate of growth of the money supply. There are of course particular deficits which will have neutral effects on financial markets at each rate of monetary growth, and therefore at each long-term inflation rate. A very brief summary of present thinking might run as follows.

If the projected real medium term growth rate of the economy is, say, $2\frac{1}{2}$ per cent per annum, then the nominal gross national product will grow at a medium term rate of $12\frac{1}{2}$ per cent if inflation is 10 per cent, $7\frac{1}{2}$ per cent if inflation is 5 per cent, and $2\frac{1}{2}$ per cent if inflation is zero. Portfolio theory suggests as a first approximation that the national debt might have a neutral effect on financial markets if its ratio to the national product remains stable. That means that a 10 per cent inflation target would be compatible with a $12\frac{1}{2}$ per cent rate of growth of the nominal national debt, a 5 per cent inflation target would be compatible with $7\frac{1}{2}$ per cent growth in the debt while a zero inflation target would entail growth in the nominal national debt of only $2\frac{1}{2}$ per cent per annum. As the national debt is now approximately 50 per cent of the British gross national product, adding to debt by $12\frac{1}{2}$ per cent per annum, which is what is permitted when inflation is 10 per cent, allows the government to borrow 50/100 times $12\frac{1}{2}$ per cent of the national income, or $6\frac{1}{4}$ per cent of the national income. Hence a public sector borrowing requirement of 6 per cent of the national income is acceptable so long as inflation of 10 per cent is tolerated. But Mrs Thatcher's government has reduced inflation to around 5 per cent and at this rate the nominal gross national product has been growing by only $7\frac{1}{2}$ per cent per annum. This has meant that the government is now able to add only 50/100 times $7\frac{1}{2}$ per cent to the national debt, which has limited the public sector borrowing requirement to $3\frac{3}{4}$ per cent of the gross national product, and this has been approximately the level of government borrowing in recent years. Mrs Thatcher's government hopes to reduce inflation to around 3 per cent by 1989, and if it succeeds in this objective, then the nominal gross national product will grow by only 5 to 6 per cent per annum. When 3 per cent inflation is attained therefore, it will only be possible to add 5 or 6 per cent per annum to the nominal national debt, so the public sector borrowing requirement will need to fall to 50/100 times 5 or 6 per cent, which comes to just $2\frac{1}{2}$ to 3 per cent of the gross national product.

Thus the gradual reduction in inflation has needed to be accompanied by a continued fall in the ratio of public sector borrowing to the national income. The Public Sector Borrowing Requirement was approximately 6 per cent when Mrs Thatcher took over in 1979, and it was reduced to 3 to 4 per cent in 1982, 1983 and 1984. It was merely 2 to 3 per cent in 1985 and 1986, so it is already low enough to prevent a rise in the ratio of government debt to the national income if inflation falls towards 3 per cent as the government hopes. There should therefore be no adverse pressures on interest rates as a result of the continued need for the government to sell public debt.

That, broadly speaking, is the thinking which lies behind the British policies with regard to the budget deficit which have been pursued in recent years. Their objective is to allow British and international portfolio holders to hold neutral ratios of British government debt in their portfolios, and the belief is that this will produce favourable interest rate behaviour, and prevent the government sector from interfering with the decisions that the private sector has to take if the British economy is to achieve a sustained recovery.

The success of these policies depends on whether the British private sector will actually achieve the investment and growth in output and employment that is needed. As Mrs Thatcher once colourfully described her strategy, she will place the ball in front of the goal for the businessmen and workers of Britain – but they and not the government will actually have to score goals. The British view is that providing these opportunities for the business community is the most that budgetary policies can hope to achieve.

4 Public Debt and Public Debt Policy in Germany

Manfred Willms

4.1 GROWTH OF PUBLIC DEBT

In post-war Germany for a long period of time public debt was not a subject of economic policy discussion. Government debt related to war-financing had been almost completely cancelled out by the currency reform of 1948, and the new constitution required a balanced budget. Debt financing was only allowed for investment purposes. Accordingly public debt grew at very moderate rates and was mainly issued by local governments. In order to stimulate private capital formation the federal budget and the state budgets for many years were in a surplus position.

This attitude towards the role of public debt changed drastically during the mid-1960s. The experience of the first post-war recession combined with a wide-spread acceptance of Keynesian ideas on stabilising economic downswings by public deficit spending led to the introduction of the 'Economic Stabilisation Law', and to an amendment of the constitution. Since then a balanced budget was not required any more. The government was allowed to run a deficit whenever a macroeconomic disequilibrium occurred. Nevertheless, the deficit was limited to the size of public investment expenditure.

For the first time in post-war Germany public debt increased by considerable amounts during the mid-1960s. However, this expansion of public debt was moderate compared to the rapid growth which took place since the mid-1970s (Figure 4.1). In 1975 public debt grew by 25 per cent. Since then the growth rates continued to be high with a slow tendency to decline in recent years. During the 11 year period from 1975 to 1985 total public debt expanded from DM 256 billion to DM 735 billion. The main responsibility for this expansion lay with the state governments (+ 252 per cent) and the federal government (+ 255 per cent). The local governments raised their debt by only 52 per cent.

Table 4.1 shows the relative economic importance of public debt and its net increase from 1964 to 1985. The table clearly indicates that

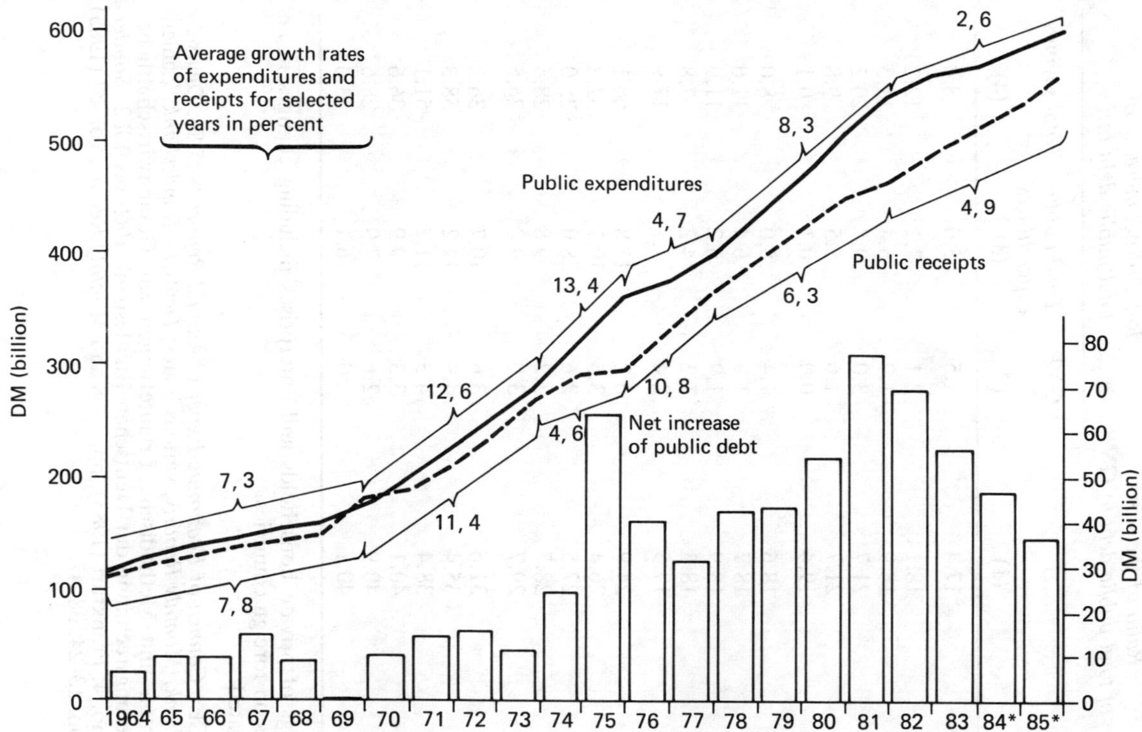

* Estimated.

SOURCE: *Deutsche Bundesbank, Monthly Reports, various issues, Council of Economic Experts, Annual Report* 1985/86.

FIGURE 4.1 *Public expenditures, public receipts and net increase of public debt, 1964–85*

TABLE 4.1 *Public debt in relation to important macroeconomic variables, 1964–85*

	Ratio of the stock of total public debt to GNP	*Ratio of net increase of total public debt to:*		
		GNP	*Total public expenditures*	*Total savings*[a]
Year	(1)	(2)	(3)	(4)
1964	17.4	1.5	5.0	8.0
1965	18.1	2.1	7.1	12.2
1966	18.9	1.9	6.4	11.3
1967	21.7	3.0	9.7	20.2
1968	21.7	1.6	5.5	9.8
1969	19.4	0.0	0.1	0.1
1970	18.6	1.4	5.0	8.0
1971	18.7	1.9	6.4	11.6
1972	18.9	1.9	6.2	11.9
1973	18.3	1.2	4.2	7.8
1974	19.5	2.4	7.7	17.9
1975	24.9	6.2	17.8	66.1
1976	26.4	3.5	10.7	32.8
1977	27.5	2.6	8.0	25.0
1978	28.7	3.2	9.8	28.4
1979	29.7	3.0	9.2	26.5
1980	31.6	3.6	10.7	36.3
1981	35.4	4.9	14.2	58.8
1982	38.4	4.3	11.2	51.1
1983	40.1	3.3	9.9	36.6
1984*	40.9	2.6	7.9	28.6
1985*	40.1	2.0	6.1	23.0

a. Savings of private households and enterprises including changes in net claims on foreign countries.

* Estimated.

SOURCE: *Council of Economic Experts, Annual Report 1985/86*, *Deutsche Bundesbank, Monthly Reports*, various issues, *Deutsche Bundesbank*, Zahlenübersichten und Methodische Erläuterungen zur Gesamtwirtschaftlichen Finanzierungsrechnung der Deutschen Bundesbank 1960 bis 1982, *Sonderdruck*, no. 4, Frankfurt (1983), pp. 44–8 and *Monthly Report*, vol. 37 (1985) no. 5, pp. 13–24, 38–47.

public debt grew much faster than nominal GNP. The ratio of total public debt to GNP rose from 17.4 per cent in 1964 to 19.5 per cent in 1974. In 1985 it reached 40.1 per cent. The ratio of public deficits to total public expenditure shows a very similar picture: with 17.8 per cent in 1975 and 14.2 per cent in 1981 extremely large portions of public expenditure have been debt-financed. However, all of these ratios do not indicate the dramatic increase in the absorption of private savings by the public sector which took place since 1975. Whilst the government sector utilised on average 11 per cent of total private savings during the 1964–74 period, it absorbed an average of 37 per cent during the 1975–85 period.

Since 1980 a growing amount of government debt has been financed by foreigners. In 1985 foreigners held more than 15 per cent of the total stock of German government debt.

4.2 CAUSES OF THE GROWTH OF PUBLIC DEBT

The growth of public debt is the outcome of a financial policy of government agencies where public expenditure continuously exceeding tax receipts. Such an economic policy can go together with a growing, a declining or an unchanged share of the government sector on GNP.

The expansion of public debt can be caused by both passive or active deficits.[1] Passive deficits are the result of cyclical fluctuations of economic activity, which occur independently of specific fiscal policy actions. They typically materialise in a period of economic downswing when the growth of tax receipts is declining while expenditures, mainly in the form of transfer payments, are increasing. Without intervention, passive deficits would vanish in a boom period when tax receipts grow faster than public expenditure. Therefore, passive deficits are economically desirable as built-in stabilisers. It is their function to cushion cyclical fluctuations of the economy. Without additional policy interventions they do not contribute to the long-run growth of public debt. Only in the case that the level of public expenditure is not adjusted to reduced rates of real economic growth passive deficits will become a long-run burden for the economy.

Active deficits are either the result of public expenditure programs in periods of business recession, or of tax cuts, or of a combination of the two. Similarly to passive deficits they raise the stock of public debt if they are not corrected by budget surpluses in boom periods.

In Germany, the rapid growth of public debt since the mid-1970s has been the outcome of both, high passive and high active deficits. Passive deficits occurred as a result of the oil-price induced recessions of 1974/75 and 1980/81, when the growth of tax receipts was declining while the growth of transfer payments was increasing. Because politically no serious effort was made to adjust the growth of welfare payments to the long-run economic possibilities, the passive deficit grew even in periods of economic recovery. Active deficits were the result of special expenditure programs aimed at reducing unemployment.[2] The programs were carried out during 1974 and 1982, more or less independently of the cyclical situation of the economy.

The policy of not correcting passive deficits and of introducing active deficits led to a considerable increase in the share of the public sector in the total economy. From 1970 to 1982 the share of public expenditure in GNP grew from 40 per cent to 52 per cent. Most of this growth was related to the social security system. Without social security, public expenditure as a percentage of GNP rose from 27 per cent in 1970 to 33 per cent in 1982.

Since the accelerated growth of public expenditure has been the main reason for the increasing stock of public debt, the question arises as to which components contributed most to the expansion of public expenditure. A breakdown of public expenditure outside the social security system is displayed in Table 4.2. The table clearly indicates the substantial change in the structure of public expenditures which took place over twenty years. From the mid-1960s to the mid-1970s the change was basically determined by an increase in the share of wages of government employees at the expense of public investments and public purchases of goods and services. Since the mid-1970s interest payments on government debt became the fastest growing component of public expenditures. Their share expanded from 4 per cent in 1975 to 9.3 per cent in 1985. During the same period, with the exception of public investments, the shares of the other types of public expenditures remained almost unchanged. The ratio of public investments declined from 21.2 per cent in 1975 to 15.8 per cent in 1985. Thus, the spending policy of the government was characterised by a restructuring of public expenditures in favour of consumption at the expense of investments.

4.3 EFFECTS OF PUBLIC DEBT ON EMPLOYMENT

The idea to fight unemployment by public deficit spending has been established and spread around the world by John Maynard Keynes in his General Theory of 1936.[3] Keynes distrusted the market forces in regaining full employment and suggested fiscal policy actions for restoring equilibrium in the labour market. According to Keynes the economic system is subject to severe fluctuations of output and employment and can remain in a disequilibrium situation for quite a while. Although Keynes does not reject the impact of wages and of the money supply on employment, he seems to relate unemployment basically to a lack of demand.

In his analysis a demand gap can occur due to psychological factors and changes in expectations which govern the demand for consumer goods, investment goods and money. A demand gap for consumer goods is explained by the 'fundamental psychological law', which implies that in the short-run the marginal propensity to consume is positive but less than unity. A demand gap for investment goods can be the outcome of a decline in the marginal efficiency of capital. The marginal efficiency of capital depends on expectations and thus is affected by waves of pessimism and optimism regarding the future course of the economy. Finally, a gap in the demand for goods and services can be the result of an increase in the demand for money, which is, besides other variables, affected by the psychological attitude towards liquidity.

In the analysis of Keynes an increase of public investment is an adequate instrument to fill the demand gap. Keynes developed the framework of the investment multiplier which shows the impact of an autonomous increase of government investment on output and thus on employment. In its simplest version the investment multiplier is dependent on the marginal propensity to consume.[4] The higher this propensity the higher is the multiplicative effect of an additional unit of government investment on real income and employment.

This rather mechanical approach neither reflects changes in relative prices nor does it include an analysis of the financing of the public deficits and its consequences. Keynes probably purposely neglected these limiting implications of his multiplier approach because he assumed rigid nominal wages and he was confronted with the problems of a deflationary economy. In a deflationary economy real income is depressed and unemployment is high because it is more attractive for investors to hold financial wealth instead of tangible capital. In such

TABLE 4.2 *Structure of public expenditures outside the social security system*

Year	*Ratio of wages of government employees to public expenditures* (1)	*Ratio of current grants to public expenditures* (2)	*Ratio of operating costs to public expenditures* (3)	*Ratio of interest payments to public expenditures* (4)	*Ratio of public investments to public expenditures* (5)
1964	26.1	21.9	20.8	2.4	28.5
1965	26.8	22.9	20.9	2.5	27.6
1966	27.7	24.4	20.3	3.0	25.1
1967	28.7	24.0	19.1	3.5	25.1
1968	29.5	24.8	18.5	3.6	24.2
1969	30.3	24.1	17.8	3.6	24.7
1970	31.3	23.9	16.3	3.5	25.4
1971	32.4	23.4	15.8	3.4	25.6
1972	32.5	24.1	15.9	3.5	23.9

1973	33.5	23.9	16.0	3.7	22.9
1974	34.2	23.9	15.6	3.9	22.6
1975	32.8	27.5	14.7	4.0	21.2
1976	33.0	27.9	14.8	4.7	19.5
1977	33.4	27.8	14.9	5.2	18.7
1978	32.5	28.2	15.1	5.0	19.2
1979	32.0	27.3	14.8	5.3	20.0
1980	31.9	27.3	14.6	5.7	20.0
1981	31.8	28.4	14.6	6.7	18.3
1982	31.9	26.4	15.3	8.0	17.5
1983	32.0	26.9	15.8	8.9	16.2
1984*	31.8	26.9	16.2	9.1	16.0
1985*	31.9	26.7	16.3	9.3	15.8

* Estimated.

SOURCE: *Federal Ministry of Finance, Financial Reports*, current issues.

an economic situation asset prices for tangible capital are too low. The easiest way to increase the price of tangible capital and to restore macroeconomic equilibrium is to increase the money stock. By recommending public deficit spending as a device for regaining full employment it was probably self-evident to Keynes that these deficits should be financed by newly issued central bank money.[5] In this case the suggested deficit spending policy turned out to be a policy of monetary stimulus.

During the nine-year period from 1974 to 1982 the economic policy of the German federal government and the state governments followed the theoretical advice given by Keynes and the Keynesians. The goal of this policy was to stabilise domestic demand and to fight unemployment. However, the result was disappointing: real domestic demand fluctuated as before and unemployment grew instead of declining. What were the reasons for this development? Why has the deficit spending policy not been able to re-establish full employment?

From an analysis of the impact of deficit spending on real domestic demand the financing of the deficit becomes highly important. If the deficit is financed by domestic savings, additional government spending will effect the interest rate and thus private spending. Whether the public demand merely crowds out private demand or whether the total effect of additional government spending on real domestic demand is positive depends on the interest elasticity of private investment demand and the interest elasticity of the demand for money.[6] A positive effect of deficit spending can only be derived by a reduced demand for money as a consequence of a deficit-induced increase in the interest rate. If the interest elasticity of money demand is large enough the additional public spending leads to a more intensive use of the existing money stock rather than a crowding out of private investment.

In a small open economy under flexible exchange rates and nearly perfect capital mobility a positive impact of bond-financed increases in government spending on real domestic demand is rather unlikely.[7] The reason for this is that the inflow of capital reduces the effect of the public deficit on the domestic interest rate and thus on the velocity of money. Under these conditions a large portion of the fiscal impetus goes to other countries. As a result, the trade account worsens together with the capital inflow. If the additional government spending is completely financed by capital imports, its effect on real domestic demand is zero. Independent of the specific models and assumptions it can be concluded that the impact of an increase of debt-financed government spending on real domestic demand is much smaller in an open economy than in a closed economy.

With the German situation it is quite obvious that public deficit spending had no consistent effect on real domestic demand. According to Figure 4.2 real domestic demand increased during periods of growing deficits – such as in 1974 and 1975 – as well as in periods of declining deficits – such as in 1982 and 1983. Nevertheless, the empirical evidence clearly indicates a close and consistent interrelationship between the growth rates of the money stock (M_1) and the growth rates of real domestic demand. Thus monetary policy seems to be a more reliable instrument for stabilising aggregate demand than a policy of public deficit spending.

The final success of public deficit policy with respect to employment does not so much depend on its impact on real domestic demand but on its impact on the differential between the profitability of private investment in tangible capital and the real rate of interest on government bonds. Recent calculations for Germany show that the rate of return on tangible capital – before taxes – decreased from about 12 per cent during the 1960s to 4 per cent in the early 1980s.[8] On the other hand there was a rise in the real rate of interest on government bonds during the 1970s and the early 1980s. As a result the rate of return differential (rate of return on capital investment minus real interest on long-term government bonds) decreased from about 8 per cent during the 1960s to less than zero per cent in the early eighties (Figure 4.2). Thus, it was more attractive for capital owners to invest in government bonds than in productive capital.

Although, since the late 1960s the decline of the profit share and of the profitability of tangible capital has been a trend phenomenon, the reduction was particularly strong after the oil price rises of 1973 and 1979/80. The main reason for the profit squeeze was the insufficient downward response of real wages to the highly negative terms-of-trade effects during 1973/74 and 1979/80/81. Thus most of the burden of the augmented oil bill was paid by the owners of tangible capital and not by labour. The only way to adjust to the cost push and profit squeeze was by a reduction of the labour force. As a result unemployment went up by almost one million in 1974/75 and by another million in 1981/82/83 (Figure 4.2). Since the profitability of productive capital never recovered its previous level, unemployment in Germany stayed high with a recent rate of 9 per cent.

Although it is somewhat questionable whether any type of fiscal policy is able to correct a fundamental disequilibrium in the labour

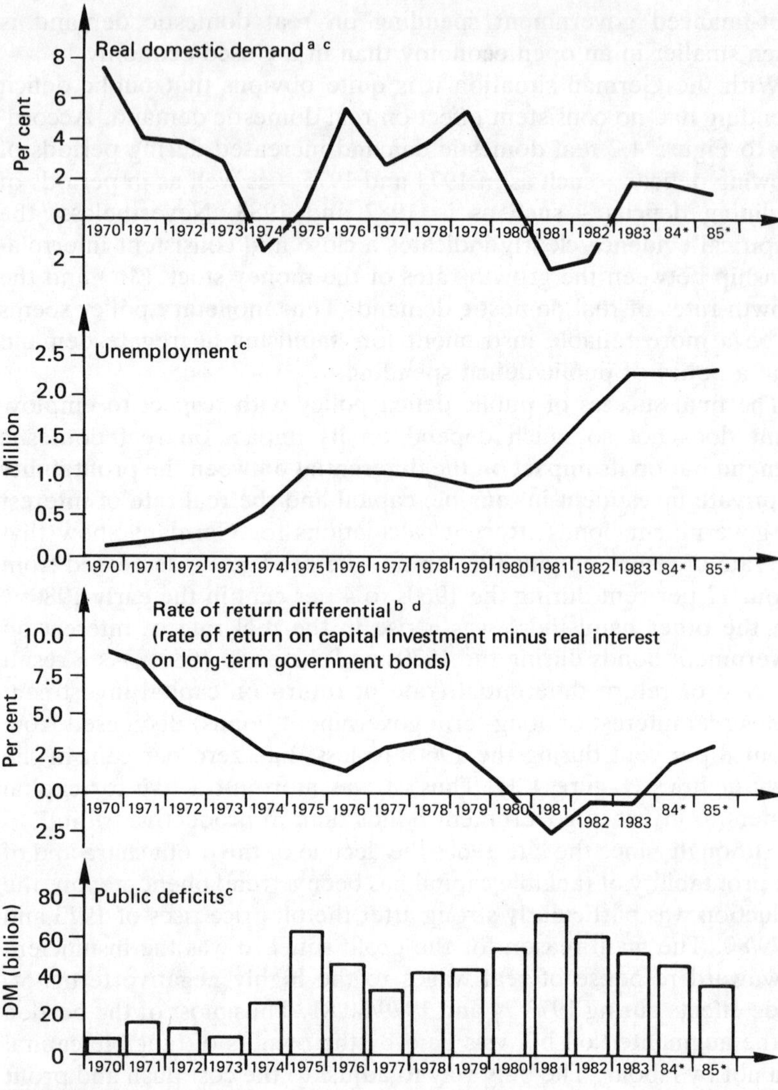

* Estimated.

SOURCES: a. *Deutsche Bundesbank, Monthly Reports*.
b. Dicke, Hugo & Peter Trapp, Zinsen. Gewinne, Nettoinvestitionen, *Kiel Institute of World Economics*, Discussion Paper no. 99, Kiel 1984.
c. *Council of Economic Experts*, *Annual Report 1985/86*.
d. The author's own calculations.

FIGURE 4.2 *Public deficits and economic activity*

market, the deficit policy carried out in Germany was just the opposite of a job creating policy. This statement is underlined by the following facts:

(1) Deficit spending increased the power of the trade unions and thus prevented the necessary wage adjustments for restoring full employment.
(2) The continuous budget deficits led to a permanent expansion of the share of (less efficient) government activity in GNP and a corresponding decline of (more efficient) private activity.
(3) An increasing section of debt-financed government expenditures went into public consumption. By this policy part of the savings capital was channelled away from job-creating private and public investments.
(4) The deficit policy was not designed to stimulate private activity in general and private investment activity in particular. Contrary to the deficit policy in the United States, in Germany tax reductions and additional tax incentives played a negligible role.

As a result, the deficit policy executed in Germany during the 1970s and early 1980s was hardly able to increase employment. In fact it may have contributed to the present unemployment situation.

4.4 EFFECTS OF PUBLIC DEBT ON INFLATION AND INTEREST RATES

An increase of public debt does not necessarily lead to inflation. Only if the growth of public debt causes an excess supply of money will inflationary pressure build up. Thus the impact of public debt on the price level depends crucially on the way a government deficit is financed. If the deficit is financed by newly issued central bank money an inflationary process is very likely to occur. However, if the deficit is financed by bonds which are absorbed by the private sector of the economy it can hardly contribute to inflation unless the central bank conducts a monetary policy of targeting the interest rate movement instead of controlling the money supply. In this case there is a tendency for the central bank to increase the money supply when bond-financed deficits put upward pressure on interest rates. Thus a policy of moderating interest rates ultimately leads to the monetisation of increases of public debt by the central bank and thereby promotes inflation.[9] With respect to its impact on inflation it is unimportant whether a deficit is directly or indirectly financed by the central bank. What matters is the final impact of the debt on the growth rate of the money stock.

Similarly to the effect of an increase of public debt on inflation, its effect on interest rates and the interest rate structure depends crucially – at least in the short run – on the way it is financed. If a deficit is financed by additional central bank money, nominal interest rates may not be affected as long as inflation has not built up. However, once inflation accrues and inflationary expectations enter the decision process of economic entities nominal interest rates will increase. Whether the rise of nominal rates influences real interest rates depends on the way inflationary expectations are formed. If inflationary expectations are generated by a learning process the adjustment to the actual rate of inflation is somewhat delayed. In this case an acceleration of the inflation rate will imply a decline of the real rate of interest while a deceleration will lead to an increasing real rate. In the case of rational expectations and a financing of the deficit via central bank money the nominal interest rate will adjust immediately to the rate of inflation. Whether and in which direction the real rate is then affected depends on the development of the total demand for credit. If the public credit demand leads to an increase in the total demand for credit the real interest rate will rise. If it merely replaces the private demand for credit the real interest rate will stay unchanged. Because in a period of recession the expected rate of return on tangible investments is rather small and private credit demand is low, budget deficits might be financed at a constant or even at a declining real interest rate. However, if budget deficits are persistently high, and thus are reflecting a shift in the time preference in favour of present consumption at the expense of future consumption, the relative scarcity of savings capital increases together with the real interest rate in the credit market. Similar effects on the nominal and the real interest rate occur when budget deficits are bond-financed.

On analysing the data for Germany (Figure 4.3) it is quite obvious that there is no systematic relationship between deficits, the money supply and inflation. The growth trend of central bank money has been influenced predominantly by foreign reserves and borrowing through the discount window and the lombard window. Public deficits definitely did not contribute to a higher growth of the money stock and never jeopardised the announced target rate of central bank money. On the contrary, for many years government debt has

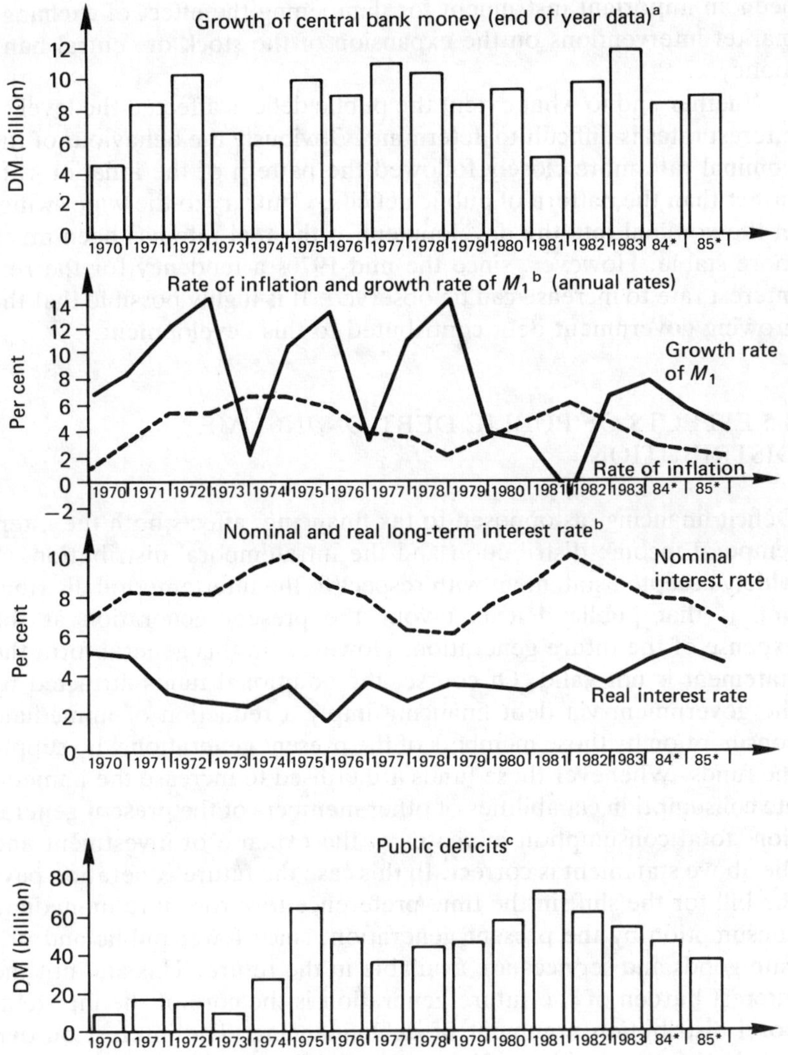

* Estimated.

SOURCES: a. *Deutsche Bundesbank, Statistische Beihefte zu den Monatsberichten*, Reihe 4.

b. *Deutsche Bundesbank, Monthly Reports.*

c. *Council of Economic Experts, Annual Report 1985/86.*

FIGURE 4.3 *Public deficits and monetary variables*

been an important instrument for dampening the effect of exchange market interventions on the expansion of the stock of central bank money.

Whether and to what extent the public deficits affected the level of interest rates is difficult to determine. Obviously the behaviour of the nominal rate more closely followed the pattern of the inflation rate rather than the pattern of public deficits. Contrary to the wide swings of the nominal rate the development of the real rate has been much more stable. However, since the mid-1970s a tendency for the real interest rate to increase can be observed. It is highly possible that the growing government debt contributed to this development.

4.5 EFFECTS OF PUBLIC DEBT ON INCOME DISTRIBUTION

Deficit financing, as opposed to tax financing, affects both the intertemporal income distribution and the intratemporal distribution. A widely accepted statement with respect to the intertemporal distribution is that public deficits favour the present generation at the expense of the future generation. However, in this general form the statement is not valid. Of course, the additional funds attracted by the government via debt financing imply a reduction of immediate consumption by those members of the present generation who supply the funds. Whenever these funds are utilised to increase the immediate consumption capabilities of other members of the present generation, total consumption increases at the expense of investment and the above statement is correct. In this case the future generation pays the bill for the shift in the time preference towards more immediate consumption by the present generation, since fewer public and private goods and services are available in the future. This and not the interest burden of the future generation is the core of the intertemporal distribution argument of debt financing. The interest burden only becomes a problem of intertemporal income distribution when it reduces the investment opportunities of the future generation.

The above argument is not valid when additional funds are transmitted, via public deficit financing, into infrastructural investments which increase the long-run productivity of the private sector of the economy. Under these conditions the future generation, on the one hand, carries the burden of the debt but, on the other hand, benefits from the advantages of the investments.

Looking at the German situation it is quite obvious that the growing government debt is reducing the income prospects of the future generation, because, as indicated before, debt financing has been a major instrument for increasing the share of public consumption and not been used to reinforce capital formation. The unsatisfactory growth performance of the German economy since the mid-1970s may be directly related to the increase of public debt. The growing interest burden, as a result of the continuous deficits, further reduces the investment opportunities of the public sector and thus affects the prospects of the younger generation.

With respect to the intratemporal distribution effect of public debt, for a long period of time the statement has been accepted that debt financing, as compared to tax financing, is advantageous to the rich at the expense of the poor. The argument is based on the assumption that government bonds are mainly held by high income people while the taxes from which the interest is paid are basically collected from low and middle income people. In this analysis, interest payments are treated as a transfer, that means a redistribution of functional income from labour to capital with the final effect of a more unequal distribution of income.

A basic limitation of the above approach is its implicit assumption that public debt financing does not lead to an increase in the interest rate. Only in this case is the functional distribution of income between capital and labour unaffected, and the analysis can be restricted to the 'transfer approach' of interest earnings. Thus the approach must be to assume that either public deficits merely replace a decline of private credit demand or that the supply of credit has been extended.

In economic reality such situations can only occur in the short-run. Private credit demand will only be low in a recession and, with a given monetary base, the banking system has only a limited short-run flexibility in its credit supply. Therefore, in the long-run, public deficits have to be financed out of private savings. Since the savings ratio of private households is fairly stable in the long-run, government borrowing must lead to an increase in the interest rate and influence the functional distribution of income.[10] This is especially true when budget deficits become a permanent phenomenon. In Germany, since the mid-1970s, public deficits have become a permanent phenomenon and therefore they contributed to a rise in the interest rate. Thus the first important assumption of the 'transfer approach' is not valid in Germany.

The second important assumption of the 'transfer approach', namely that the poor and middle income people pay most of the taxes while government bonds are mainly held by the rich, does not reflect the reality in Germany. In Germany, it is not the poor but the middle and high income people who contribute the largest share to tax receipts. Government debt, on the other hand, is to a large extent financed via direct credits from the commercial banking system. Savings- and loan- associations and private banks hold two-thirds of the government debt while the rest is held by private households, companies, foreigners and the Deutsche Bundesbank. The commercial banking system receives most of its funds from low and middle income people. Thus most of the interest payments on public debt goes to this group. As a result, intratemporal distribution effects are either non-existent or they are of negligible magnitude.[11] With the present empirical knowledge, at least, no final conclusion can be drawn with respect to the impact of public debt financing on the personal as well as on the functional income distribution.[12]

4.6 THE PRESENT POLICY OF REDUCING THE GROWTH OF PUBLIC DEBT

In the meantime, in Germany, the negative economic effects of a rapidly growing public debt have become so apparent that a broad political consensus has developed to reduce the budget deficits. Since 1982 the new government has actively persued a policy of deficit reduction. The strategy followed was basically a reduction of the growth rate of public expenditures.[13] Incentives to stimulate private economic activity via general tax reductions and specifically via a reduction of the tax burden of the business sector have only been introduced on a minor scale. The result of this policy has been a decline of the share of government expenditures from 52 per cent of GNP to 48 per cent, while the share of taxes of GNP has remained unchanged at a level of 46 per cent including social security contributions. In order to counter the automatic increase of the tax burden due to progression a tax reform is planned for 1986. However, this reform will not include tax incentives for business investment. In this respect the debt policy in Germany is quite contrary to the one carried out in the United States where massive tax cuts for households and business contributed to an increase in the public debt but at the time stimulated the strong recovery of the economy.

NOTES

1. Tatom, John A., 'A Perspective on the Federal Deficit Problem', *Federal Reserve Bank of St. Louis Review*, vol. 66, no. 6 (1984), pp. 5–17.
2. Willms, Manfred & Ingo Karsten, 'Government Policies towards Inflation and Unemployment: Experience in Germany', in Argy, Victor & John Neville (eds), *Inflation and Unemployment, Theory, Experience and Policy Making* (London, 1985).
3. Keynes, John Maynard, *The General Theory of Employment, Interest and Money* (London 1936), chapter 18.
4. Keynes, John Maynard, *The General Theory of Employment, Interest and Money*, op. cit., chapter 9.
5. At least this conclusion can be drawn by a careful analysis of the work of Keynes. See for example Leijonhuf vud Axel, *On Keynesian Economics and the Economics of Keynes* (New York, London, Toronto, 1968), chapter VI, 2.
6. For a theoretical analysis of these effects and of the recent crowding-out discussion see Siebke, Jürgen, Dieter Knoll and Wolf-Dieter Schmidberger, 'Theoretische Grundlagen des crowding-out Effekts', in Ehrlicher, Werner (ed.), *Geldpolitik, Zins und Staatsverschuldung, Schriften des Vereins für Socialpolitik*, vol. 111 (Berlin, 1981), pp. 227–62.
7. Mundell, Robert A, *International Economics* (New York, 1968); see also: Lehment, Harmen, The Macroeconomic Implications of Public Sector Deficits, Kiel Institute of World Economics, Working Paper no. 168 (Kiel, 1983).
8. Dicke, Hugo & Peter Trapp, Zinsen, Gewinne, Nettoinvestitionen, Kiel Institute of World Economics, Discussion Paper no. 99 (Kiel, 1984).
9. This type of interrelationship between deficits and inflation has been frequently observed in the United States. See Hamburger, Michael J. & Burton Zwick, Deficits, Money and Inflation, *Journal of Monetary Economics*, vol. 7 (1981), pp. 141–50.
10. Gandenberger, Otto, 'Theorie der öffentlichen Verschuldung', in: Neumark, Fritz (ed.), *Handbuch der Finanzwissenschaft* (Tübingen, 1981), p. 39.
11. Willms, Manfred, 'Volkswirtschaftliche Wirkungen einer zunehmenden Staatsverschuldung', in *Wirtschaftsdienst*, vol. 58 (1978), pp. 439–45.
12. Gandenberger, Otto, 'Theorie der öffentlichen Verschuldung', op. cit., p. 41.
13. For a discussion of various possible strategies see *Wissenschaftlicher Beirat beim Bundesministerium der Finanzen*, Gutachten zu den Problemen einer Verringerung der öffentlichen Netto-Neuverschuldung (Bonn, 1984), pp. 25–38.

5 Public Finance and Monetary Policy in Italy (1973–83): Trends and Problems

Terenzio Cozzi

5.1 GENERAL REMARKS

Among industrial countries, Italy is perhaps the one with the worst record in public finance. A few data will suffice to illustrate the statement. In 1983, the public administrations' expenditure went to 57.3 per cent of GDP. In the EEC countries the same figure averaged 52.0 per cent. As for total revenue, the data are: 45.5 per cent for Italy and 46.6 per cent for the EEC (Table 5.1). This greater expenditure corresponded to a lower revenue and, therefore, a much larger deficit: 11.8 per cent as against 5.4 per cent. The 1983 result is not an isolated one. In the period 1981–83, the Italian deficit averaged more than 12.1 per cent, while in the EEC it averaged less than 5.3 per cent.

Moreover, we have to recall that public administrations represent a smaller aggregate than the public sector, not to mention the enlarged public sector. They do not include the autonomous state enterprises (Railways, Post and Telegraph, State Telephone, and Tobacco monopoly) that belong to the public sector, and the State Electricity Company that belongs to the enlarged public sector. In 1983, the public sector borrowing requirement (PSBR) reached 17.0 per cent and that of the enlarged public sector 17.4 per cent of the GDP (Table 5.2).

Propelled by such large borrowing requirements, the stock of public debt rocketed to unprecedented levels in peace times: in 1983 it rose to 84.6 per cent of the GDP from 70.0 per cent in 1981. Over the same period, in the seven largest industrial countries of the OECD, the ratio of debt to GDP increased on average by less than 7 per cent points to 50.8 per cent.[1]

Three years of economic recession obviously contributed to the

TABLE 5.1 *Public administrations: international comparisons (% of GDP)*

	1979	*1980*	*1981*	*1982*	*1983*
Current revenue					
Italy	35.9	38.1	39.6	42.8	45.5
EEC	40.6	43.8	44.6	45.7	46.6
Total expenditure					
Italy	45.4	45.9	51.3	54.7	57.3
EEC	44.0	47.3	49.8	50.9	52.0
Deficit					
Italy	9.5	8.0	11.9	12.7	11.8
EEC	3.4	3.5	5.2	5.2	5.4

SOURCE: Bank of Italy, *Relazione 1983*, p. 135.

TABLE 5.2 *Borrowing requirements (% of GDP)*

	1979	*1980*	*1981*	*1982*	*1983*	*1984*	*1985**
Public Sector	11.8	12.4	13.3	16.3	17.0	16.7	17.5
Enlarged Public Sect.	12.3	13.2	13.6	17.0	17.4	17.4	

* Estimated, Bank of Italy, *Bollettino Economico*, no. 5, Oct. 1985, p. 30.

SOURCE: Bank of Italy, *Relazione 1983, Appendice*, pp. 46–7, 124; *Relazione 1984*, p. 131.

worsening of the public finance situation. But, according to OECD estimations, their effect on the increase of the PSBR to GDP ratio is measured by 1.5 percentage points in 1983, and by 1.0 and by 0.4 points respectively in the two previous years. Something similar happened in other countries but their performance was not as bad as the Italian one.[2]

Structural forces making for greater and greater public deficits are at work in Italy, and they are much stronger than in other industrial countries. So far it has proved impossible to slow down the growth of the public expenditure in excess of that of GDP. The whole burden of avoiding a still greater worsening of public deficits fell on revenue, which in fact increased a lot but not sufficiently.

In the absence of drastic changes in the legal provisions that determine, mainly in the social sector, the growth of expenditure net of interest, the prospects look very gloomy. There is an inherent tendency for this expenditure to grow much faster than GDP. The servicing of a very large and rapidly increasing debt – with a real rate of interest higher than the foreseable real rate of growth for GDP, will strongly accelerate the already quick expansion of total expenditure. The task of avoiding the explosion of the deficit by increasing public revenue as fast as over the recent past, or even faster, seems to be not only impossible but also undesirable.

It is sufficient to point out that in Italy there is a very large tax evasion by self-employed workers and by receivers of unearned income. On the other hand, the taxation of employees is considered too high not only by the workers and their unions, but also by the Government. Therefore, any success in reducing evasion should be partially matched by a reduction in the workers' relative tax burden. However, one has also to recall that the current public administrations' revenue was at 45.5 per cent of GDP in 1983. The average ratio for the EEC was 46.6 per cent. But, *per capita* income is much lower in Italy than in the EEC. If it is true that, given the growing needs of public finance, the weight of taxation cannot be reduced but has to be increased, it is also true that it will be very hard to lift the workers' burden. In any case, only a drastic slowing down of expenditure growth could start a process of redressing the Italian public finance.

5.2 THE GROWTH OF EXPENDITURE

Let us have a closer look at the causes that brought about the present gloomy situation. Public sector current expenditure rose, as a proportion of GDP, from 37 per cent in 1974 to 54.7 per cent in 1983 (Table 5.3). All the main expenditure items played their part in the rise. The fastest growing item, both relatively and absolutely, was that of the interest payments. Its ratio to GDP almost trebled: from 3.3 per cent in 1974 to 9.2 per cent in 1983. Particularly impressive was the increase of 3 full points in the last three years. The causes are not only to be found in the ever growing stock of debt and in the recessive conditions that slowed down the denominator of the ratio. As we shall see later on, another important cause comes from the Bank of Italy's decision to reduce drastically the monetary financing of public debt. The nominal interest rates registered a huge rise in 1981, while inflation started to decline. In the two years following they had been reduced, but only in line with the falling inflation or a bit less. As a

TABLE 5.3 *Public sectors expenditure (% of GDP)*

	1974	*1975*	*1976*	*1977*	*1978*	*1979*	*1980*	*1981*	*1982*	*1983*	*1984*
Wages and salaries	13.1	13.1	12.6	13.1	13.6	13.9	14.1	15.9	16.0	16.4	16.4
Purchase of goods and services	5.0	5.4	4.9	5.0	5.1	5.3	5.2	5.7	6.1	6.5	6.6
Social security and welfare	13.7	15.7	15.6	15.2	16.5	15.7	15.8	17.7	18.7	20.0	19.5
Transfers to enterprises	0.9	1.3	1.5	1.5	1.7	1.5	1.4	1.3	1.7	1.8	1.7
Interest payments	3.3	4.2	4.7	5.1	6.0	5.9	6.4	7.3	8.6	9.2	9.9
Other expenditure	0.9	1.0	1.0	1.0	1.2	0.7	0.7	0.7	1.0	0.7	0.8
Current expenditure	37.0	40.7	40.3	40.9	44.1	43.1	43.6	48.7	52.0	54.7	54.8
Capital expenditure	4.3	5.4	5.0	5.0	5.0	5.0	5.2	5.7	6.1	6.7	7.3
Total expenditure	41.3	46.1	45.3	45.9	49.1	48.1	48.8	54.4	58.2	61.4	62.1

SOURCE: Bank of Italy, *Relazione, Appendice*, 1983–84.

result, the real rates, that before were largely negative, became positive and very high.

The next item with the fastest growth was social security expenditure. The transfers to households, either in money or in kind, increased from 13.7 per cent to 20.0 per cent over the decade. Of this increase, 4.2 points have been recorded in the last three years. It should, nevertheless, be emphasised that social security transfers declined slightly over the decade (from 37.1 per cent to 36.5 per cent) as a proportion of total current expenditure.

There are some indications that the most rapidly growing items in the total transfers were pensions, both to public employees and to disabled people, and health expenditure. The pensions to public employees had been propelled by a long-standing privilege that allows them to become pensioners while still very young, and to cumulate the State pension with a new wage or salary income. Since there were repeated rumours of a possible repeal of this privilege, many public employees decided to become pensioners.

Expenditure on pensions for disabled people grew very quickly during the 1970s owing to the increase in the number of entitled persons, many of whom in fact were not disabled at all. It seems that in many cases pensions were used as a substitute for the scarcity of jobs, mainly in the depressed areas. As a consequence of a tighter surveillance and of changes in laws regulating the right to pension allowance, the growth of this expenditure has slowed down over recent years.

Contrary to this, during the period 1975–1980, pension payments to old age workers of the private sectors do not seem to have grown faster than GDP, notwithstanding the aging of the population. The average earnings did not keep full pace with inflation. But afterwards the situation changed completely. Quicker indexation and the revaluation of most pension allowances brought about expenditure increases that were much higher than GDP growth. The prospects are alarming. The ratio of old age to active population, that was 40 per cent in 1971 and 42 per cent in 1981, is expected to rise to 45 per cent in 1991 and further afterwards. The number of pensioners is expected to increase by roughly 1 per cent per year from now on. Moreover, owing mainly to periods of contribution greater than in the past, the average earnings of the pensioners are expected to rise, in real terms, at a rate of a 1–1.5 per cent higher than the earnings of active workers.[3]

As for health expenditures, they grew not only to cater for the greater needs of an increasingly aged population but also, and perhaps foremost, as a consequence of an institutional change that transferred to lower government levels responsibility for administrating health expenditures, but not that of providing for the financial cover. In fact, it is fair to point out that, in this as in other cases, the decentralisation of the expenditure decisions coupled with the centralisation of the levying power has greatly enhanced financial irresponsibility in many areas of public activity.

The expenditure on wages and salaries rose from 13.1 per cent of GDP to 16.4 per cent, roughly in line with the increase in the proportion of the public sector to total employment. But the path was different in different periods. Up to 1980, the high growth of the number of employees, propelled during the first years by a change in the political colour of many local administrations, was largely counteracted by lowered average real wages relative to private employment. Contrary to this, in the years 1983–85, the number of employees still expanded at a fairly high rate, but unitary real wages rose considerably faster than earnings in the private sector. As a result, we had an increase of 2.3 points in the ratio of public expenditure on wages and salaries to GDP, more than double the increase of the previous seven years. It is obvious that you cannot rely for long on the possibility of compressing the real earnings of public (or, for that matter, any) employees, as against those of other workers. The most likely result of such a course is that, sooner or later, a wage–wage spiral will take place. This is precisely what happened in Italy with public sector wages and also, as we had already seen, with pensions.

The story of the other expenditure items can be told very briefly. The purchase of goods and services rose in the decade 1975–85 from 5.0 per cent to 6.5 per cent. Its share in total current expenditure fell from 13.5 per cent to 11.9 per cent. The figures are not very large and this is one of the factors explaining the small value of the Keynesian multiplier of public expenditure in Italy.[4] The demand going directly to productive sectors is in fact rather small.

Also the capital expenditure rose faster than GDP. It passed from 4.3 per cent to 6.7 per cent (Table 5.3). But this increase does not correspond to an equal increase in the gross capital formation. In fact, a large amount of capital expenditure is nothing other than the cover of previous losses incurred by public enterprises.

It is well to notice that, of the total public expenditure net of interest, in 1983 almost 70 per cent went to households as wages, pensions and other social security transfers. The rest went to the productive sectors in various forms: public works, purchases of goods and services, subsidies, financing of public enterprises and so on. The expenditure going to households is directly indexed to wages; that going to productive sectors is indexed indirectly, via the ensuing inflation. The interest payments have a behaviour of their own, being propelled by increasing debt and by nominal interest rates maintained high by inflation and by restrictive monetary policies. This means that the prospects of slowing down expenditure growth have to be found in a severe incomes policy, rather than in the possibility of drastically reducing some items of existing expenditure. In this latter respect, it seems that measures of rationalisation are strongly and urgently required to improve the very poor quality of the services provided. In the process, some savings may prove possible, – not so large in the short run perhaps and considerable only after fairly long delays. Rationalisation is not an alternative to incomes policy, it is a necessary complement to it.

5.3 THE PATH OF REVENUE

The total revenue of the public sectors increased very rapidly during the decade 1974–83. Its ratio to GDP rose from 33.1 per cent to 47.5 per cent (Table 5.4), a record among OECD countries. Particularly relevant was the growth over the last three years: almost 3 percentage points of GDP per year.

The largest increase, both relatively and absolutely, occurred in direct taxation whose ratio to GDP rose from 6.3 per cent to 15.5 per cent. Next to it there is the growth of social contributions, which passed from 12.8 per cent to 16.3 per cent. Indirect taxation grew rather less: from 9.8 per cent to 11.2 per cent, all the increase being obtained in the last two years. The receipts from the sale of goods and services went up and down before increasing a little in the last three years when, at last, some significant rises in public fares was decided. The other minor items or receipts remained constant in relative terms.

The first thing to point out is that Italy started in 1974 with a very low proportion of direct taxation to total revenue: 19 per cent, almost equal to that of France but far lower than those of the UK, USA, Germany, Japan, etc . . . During the following decade, while in the other countries the proportion of direct taxation remained constant,

TABLE 5.4 *Public sectors revenue (% of GDP)*

	1974	*1975*	*1976*	*1977*	*1978*	*1979*	*1980*	*1981*	*1982*	*1983*	*1984*
Direct taxation	6.3	6.7	7.9	8.7	10.1	9.9	11.2	12.8	14.2	15.5	15.3
Indirect taxation	9.8	8.8	9.6	10.3	10.1	9.4	10.1	9.7	10.1	11.2	11.3
Social contributions	12.8	14.0	14.0	13.8	14.0	14.5	14.5	14.7	15.7	16.3	16.2
Property income	0.9	0.7	0.7	0.7	0.8	0.9	0.9	0.9	0.9	0.8	0.7
Sales of goods and services	2.2	2.3	2.5	2.4	2.4	2.3	2.0	2.2	2.3	2.5	2.5
Other revenue	0.9	0.9	0.8	0.8	1.0	1.0	1.0	1.2	1.0	1.0	1.1
Current revenue	32.9	33.5	35.4	36.6	38.3	37.9	39.7	41.6	44.3	47.3	47.2
Capital revenue	0.2	0.2	0.2	0.6	0.2	0.1	0.2	0.2	0.2	0.2	0.2
Total Revenue	33.1	33.6	35.6	37.1	38.4	38.0	39.9	41.7	44.4	47.5	47.4

SOURCE: Bank of Italy, *Relazione, Appendice*, 1983–84.

or declined a little, in Italy it increased very quickly up to 32.6 per cent in 1983. The difference between the high direct taxation countries almost disappeared.

The contrary happened with indirect taxation. It was fairly high in 1974, only France having a higher proportion to total revenue. By 1983, Italy has become one of the countries, perhaps the country, with the lowest indirect taxation (23.6 per cent of the total revenue).

Such big changes in the structure of taxation did not make the Italian system more equitable. Perhaps it became more iniquitous, owing to the already mentioned large evasion both of direct and indirect taxation. It is no surprise that dissatisfaction is increasing so rapidly as to evoke fears that it might soon become a threat to democracy, as a former minister of finance once said.

The social contributions still represent a higher proportion of total receipts than in other countries, with the exception of France which had a considerable proportionate increase over the last two decades. In Italy their contribution to total revenue fell from 38.8 per cent to 34.3 per cent. The possibility of further reductions seems to be precluded by mounting public deficits. Some time ago, it was suggested that social contributions be reduced in order to improve the competitiveness of Italian exporters without directly fuelling a greater inflation, as happens with devaluation. Some reductions have actually been implemented in the past. But now this road seems no longer open.

If one thinks over the very high growth of public revenue, one cannot help concluding that it was the inability to slow down expenditure that is responsible for the disastrous state of public finance, not the inability to speed up taxation. Moreover, taking into account the fact that already almost half of the GDP goes as public revenue, one has to consider that such a burden falls on incomes that, on average, they are much lower than in other industrial countries. Some politicians say that Italy is not very far from becoming a socialist country in disguise. It is only fair to add that one big difference still remains: that rich people are only slightly affected by the tax system, which should not happen with ideal socialism.

5.4 PUBLIC DEFICITS, SAVINGS AND INVESTMENT

The consequences of the growing public sectors' imbalances are very far reaching. The first thing to point out is that large deficits will be recorded even before taking account of investment expenditure. They are already present in the current accounts, which means that a considerable part of the private savings has to be used not to finance investment but to finance the public sectors' current activity, i.e. their consumption. Hence such a part of the private savings is literally destroyed. It no longer appears in the national accounts of capital formation; it is taken away by the public sectors' negative savings.

The case of Italy is unique among industrial countries. In almost all of them the public sectors' current account usually shows a surplus; not very large but a surplus. There have been some exceptions. The recent experience of the USA is the most important and there are already signs that it will quite soon prove unsustainable. Another important exception was that of the UK in the late 1970s. But, in this case, the imbalance was temporary and fairly quickly reversed. Contrary to this, the Italian public sectors have registered large negative savings since the beginning of the 1970s. Moreover, the trend is worsening, apart from oscillations. In 1974 the negative saving was equal to 3.5 per cent of GDP; in 1983 it came to 6.4 per cent while the year before it was 7.2 per cent (Table 5.5). In the years 1981–84, and in 1975, the public sectors' current deficit destroyed more than $\frac{1}{3}$ of the total gross savings recorded in national accounts. It will be no surprise to learn that the ratio of savings to GDP, that in the past was far above 20 per cent, fell below this level since 1981 and reached a minimum of 17.9 per cent in 1983. It has not fallen even more because of the high propensity of households to save that stayed well above 20 per cent of their disposable income. Among the reasons explaining such a high saving propensity, it is well to consider the previously mentioned large margins of fiscal evasion and also the tax exemption of all the interests accruing to households on their holdings of public debt. Both these elements seem to be important for the rich households that save a high proportion of their income.

The contribution of households to gross national saving in the years 1981–84 was about 110 per cent. The enterprises and financial institutions contributed more or less another 27 per cent, while the public sectors reduced the total by 37 per cent. If one attributes the savings of family enterprises to the households, the latter's contribution has to be increased by approximately 10 per cent. This rough calculation leaves the savings of the enterprises and financial institutions at 17 per cent, which is almost the percentage to be attributed to banks and insurance companies alone. In practice, very little was left as corporate saving, i.e. as undistributed profits (net of losses).[5] It is

TABLE 5.5 *Sources of savings; investments % of GDP (current prices)*

	Households	*Enterprises and private social institutes*	*Banks and insurance companies*	*Public administrations*	*Gross savings*	*Gross investment*	*External current balance*
1974	19.8	4.3	1.3	–3.5	21.9	26.5	–4.6
1975	23.0	1.7	2.2	–6.8	20.1	20.3	–0.2
1976	22.1	2.8	2.0	–4.8	22.1	23.6	–1.5
1977	21.7	2.9	2.0	–4.0	22.6	21.4	+1.2
1978	22.9	2.6	2.3	–5.4	22.4	20.0	+2.4
1979	21.9	3.8	2.4	–5.1	23.0	21.3	+1.7
1980	19.9	3.4	2.6	–3.4	22.5	25.0	–2.5
1981	20.4	2.4	3.1	–6.8	19.0	21.3	–2.3
1982	20.6	2.5	2.5	–7.2	18.5	20.1	–1.6
1983	19.4	2.0**	2.9	–6.4	17.9	17.7	+0.2
1984	19.0*			–6.8*	17.7*	18.6*	–0.9*

% of gross savings (current prices)

1974	90.2	19.5	6.2	–15.9	100	121.2	–21.2
1975	114.8	8.3	10.6	–33.7	100	101.1	– 1.1
1976	99.9	12.8	9.1	–21.8	100	106.8	– 6.8
1977	96.2	12.7	8.8	–17.7	100	94.8	+ 5.1
1978	102.4	11.5	10.3	–24.2	100	89.4	+10.6
1979	95.2	16.6	10.4	–22.2	100	92.6	+ 7.4
1980	88.2	15.3	11.7	–15.2	100	110.9	–10.9
1981	107.3	12.5	16.3	–36.1	100	112.3	–12.3
1982	111.4	13.5	13.5	–38.9	100	108.6	– 8.6
1983	108.4	11.2**	16.2	–35.8	100	98.9*	+ 1.1
1984	107.3*			–38.4	100	105.1*	– 5.1*

* Provisional.
**Estimated.

SOURCE: Bank of Italy, *Relazione*.

true that the years 1981–83 were marked by a severe recession and that, subsequently, the enterprises' financial situation has improved a lot. But it is also true that, apart from oscillations, the trend of corporate profits as a ratio to GDP has been downwards since the beginning of the 1970s. And it had consequences on the propensity to invest that also pointed downwards.

Contrary to this, the savings (and profits) of the financial institutions increased, as a ratio to GDP, from less than 2 per cent a decade ago to almost 3 per cent now. As we shall see later on, the good results of the banks had been favoured by some measures of monetary policy that were decided in order to make easier the financing of the public sectors. But the private ones had to pay for it in terms of higher cost of credit.

The same picture emerges if we consider the flows of the sectoral financial balances inclusive of the expenditure for real investment (Table 5.6). The households' surplus, while oscillating, remained pretty high: in the range 15–16 per cent of GDP over the last few years. The deficit of the public sectors rose almost uninterruptedly from 10.0 per cent in 1976 to 14.5 per cent over the years 1983–84. As a consequence, there remained little room for the financial needs of the private sectors. Notwithstanding the relevant surpluses of banks and financial institutions and of sectors not classifiable elsewhere, the domestic financing of investments proved possible only when they were at their lowest.

A comparison between the figures for 1978 and 1982 will suffice to illustrate the point. The sum of internal surpluses (of households, banks, etc.) in 1981 was higher than in 1978 by 0.7 per cent of GDP. The deficit of the enterprises was almost at the same level in both years. But the public sectors' deficit was higher by more than 4 percentage points. As a result, in 1982 we had a current balance of payments deficit of 1.5 per cent of GDP, while in 1978 we had a surplus of 2.4 per cent.

It seems that the growing pressure on real resources exercised by the public sectors is at the origin of the balance of payments difficulties that appear as soon as the productive firms resume their investments. Restrictive monetary policies then become unavoidable. Their consequences fall mainly on productive firms, so hampering the growth of production. But they also fall on the public budget, by increasing interest payments and social transfers and by decreasing the receipts from taxation. Therefore, more resources are needed by the public sectors. But they are not provided by the private ones that are kept in

TABLE 5.6 *Financial balances (% of GDP)*

		Households	*Enterprises*	*Banks, fin. inst., not included elsewhere**	*Public sectors*	*Rest of the world*
Old series	1974	12.7	–7.9	0.3	– 9.8	4.7
	1975	16.5	–7.7	3.3	–12.4	0.3
New series	1976	13.9	–8.3	2.9	–10.0	1.5
	1977	13.9	–4.0	0.4	– 9.2	–1.1
	1978	15.6	–3.6	0.7	–10.3	–2.4
	1979	14.3	–2.4	0.0	–10.2	–1.7
	1980	12.2	–7.6	3.1	–10.1	2.4
	1981	13.8	–6.2	3.7	–13.6	2.3
	1982	14.6	–3.9	2.5	–14.7	1.5
	1983	16.3	–4.4	2.6	–14.3	–0.2
	1984	16.7	–4.0	2.1	–15.6	0.8

* Calculated as the balancing item.

SOURCE: Bank of Italy, *Relazione*, various years.

check by monetary restrictions. We are in a vicious circle. The only way to break it depends on the possibility of reducing the public expenditure as a proportion to GDP.

5.5 DEFICIT FINANCING AND MONETARY POLICY

It is obvious that, in the context outlined, very difficult problems had to be faced by monetary authorities. Two of them were most worrying: the weakness of the balance of payments and the necessity of assuring the continuous financing of a rapidly growing public debt. In connection with these, there was also the imperative need of avoiding a possible reduction in the households' propensity to save and of inducing them to continuously increase their holdings of public debt.

According to the prevailing view at the Bank of Italy, 'during the 70's the disequilibria in the industrial countries stemming from the raw material and labour markets, as well as high and variable inflation rates, undermined the use of interest rates as intermediate objectives, and encouraged the increasingly widespread use of monetary and credit aggregates for this purpose'.[6] Consequently, since the beginning of the 1970s, the Bank of Italy chose as its intermediate objective a broad financial aggregate: the Total Domestic Credit Expansion (TDCE).[7] It seemed to be the only sensible choice for a country with a most stringent external constraint. In fact, a contraction of the TDCE will force firms both to seek greater financing on the international markets and to reduce the level of inventories and production. The effects on the balance of payments will clearly be favourable. And also they will come rather quickly, owing to the very large indebtment of the Italian enterprises with the banks. The transmission mechanics will operate directly from the financial to the real markets, with somewhat high degrees of rapidity and precision.

Every year the Bank of Italy fixed a target, not announced officially, for the TDCE. But, most of the time the actual expansion was much greater than the targeted one (see Table 5.7). In fact, given the very fast growth of the PSBR, to maintain the TDCE at the fixed targets would have meant that private sectors could not find the necessary credit even for their current activity, not to mention investments.

As an illustration, let us consider the case of 1983. The targets were: 105 billion lira for the total expansion, of which 65 billion should have gone to the public and 40 billion to the private sectors.

TABLE 5.7 *GDP, prices, money and credit indicators*

	Growth of GDP (real)	*Growth of GDP (nominal)*	*GDP deflator rate of growth*	*Consumer prices rate of growth*	*M2 rate of growth*	*TDCE targets*	*TDCE realised*	*PSDC TDC %*	*PSDCE TDCE %*
1974	4.1	22.6	17.6	19.1	15.3	18.1	17.3	40.2	41.2
1975	–3.6	13.2	17.5	17.0	23.5	17.0	21.5	41.2	45.7
1976	5.9	24.9	17.9	16.7	21.2	16.8	19.3	41.3	41.7
1977	1.9	21.3	19.2	17.0	21.6	14.6	16.8	42.7	50.8
1978	2.7	16.9	13.9	12.1	20.6	15.5	20.1	46.3	64.2
1979	4.9	21.6	15.9	14.8	20.4	18.0	18.2	47.3	53.0
1980	3.9	25.4	20.6	21.2	13.4	17.0	18.1	48.3	53.8
1981	0.2	18.5	18.4	17.8	12.5	15.7	17.7	50.3	61.5
1982	–0.5	17.4	17.9	16.5	17.3	15.1	20.7	53.5	68.7
1983	–0.4	13.7	15.0	14.7	12.6	17.9	20.5	56.5	71.4
1984	2.6	13.6	10.7	10.8	12.5		19.5		

SOURCE: Bank of Italy, *Relazione*, various years; C. Caranza & A. Fazio, *Methods of Monetary Control*.

But the actual absorption by the public sectors was 85.6 billion. Therefore, in order not to exceed the overall target, the private sectors should have received less than 20 billion, i.e. less than half of what was originally planned. And this is already a much lower amount, in real terms, than that obtained the year before. What happened was that the private sectors had been actually squeezed, but by a smaller amount. They, in fact, received 34.2 billion, 14.5 per cent less than had originally been established. But the TDCE went up to 119.8 billion, thus exceeding the initial target by more than 14 per cent.

The Bank of Italy had a very hard task in trying to avoid both too drastic a squeeze of the private sectors and a TDCE too large to keep the balance of payments in order. The difficulties increased with the increase of the share of TDCE going to the public sectors. In 1974 this share was 41.2 per cent; in 1983 it was 71.4 per cent. The private sector got the differences from 100. While at the beginning of the period, it was still possible to compensate a moderate surpassing of the public sectors' targeted credit with a moderate reduction of that going to private sectors, this was no longer possible at the end of the period, as is clearly shown by the 1983 case. The power to control the aggregate demand through the control of TDCE was greatly reduced. Correspondingly, the Bank of Italy started to give less and less importance to TDCE as the single, or most prominent, intermediate objective, and to give more and more importance to the control of monetary base and of money M2.

But the change in intermediate objectives, from the control of a broad credit aggregate to a rather narrow monetary aggregate, has other explanations too. Moreover, as will be apparent in a moment, this change was not the only one and, perhaps, not the one with the most far reaching consequences.

In fact, during the 1970s, the control of TDCE was realised mainly through *administrative* measures. In particular, they 'relied heavily on the use of ceilings for bank credit expansion'.[8] This instrument of direct control became more and more pervasive with the passage of time. It started with the aim of limiting only the loans of large amounts denominated in lira. But, sooner or later, the total of all loans offered by Italian banks, both large and small, both in lira and in foreign currencies, had to be kept below the ceiling. But, as always happens, the stricter the controls the greater the efforts of avoiding them by expanding forms of loans not yet controlled and by introducing some new ones. The TDCE became more and more uncontrollable. Its relation to the final objectives became less precise than it used to be. A given value of TDCE appeared to be consistent with different degrees of actual monetary restriction. Moreover, the growth of monetary base and of money M2, not under control, very often grew faster than was considered safe by the Bank of Italy.

The mechanism of the ceilings forced the banks to increase their holdings of public debt, so easing its non-monetary financing. The private sectors were rationed both quantitatively and by a greater cost of lending. On the other hand, the rate of interest on Treasury bills stood lower than it would otherwise have, and much lower than the rate of inflation. Still lower, and by large amounts, stood the interest rates paid by the banks on households' deposits. Hence, there was a strong inducement to change the composition of households' portfolios', in favour of Treasury bills and against bank and other deposits which, in the late 1970s represented a very high proportion (over 60 per cent) of their total financial wealth (Table 5.8).

For a number of years during the 1970s, the direct monetary control made it possible to issue on the market very large amounts of public securities offering a highly negative real interest rate. But it proved impossible to fund the whole of the PSBR in this way. A large part of it had to be financed in monetary base. The Bank of Italy was at risk of losing its monetary sovereignty.

One of the reasons, but not the only one, was the small scope, or the almost non-existence, of a well organised money market. The Bank of Italy consistently operated with the aim of creating one – and with rather good results, given the point of departure. Households started more and more to approach the market, first by buying Treasury bills (BOT) and then also large amounts of Treasury Credit Certificates (CCT), i.e. medium term bonds yielding an interest rate indexed to that of the six-monthly Treasury bills. In 1974 these funds had no part in the total households' financial assets. In 1983 they came to count for more than 22 per cent of the stock, and for more than 45 per cent of the change, of the households' financial wealth (Table 5.8).

The development of a market with such a large participation of households as buyers, was a pre-condition for another important institutional change. For many years, the Bank of Italy had been obliged to assure the selling of the total amount of securities issued by the Treasury. What was not possible to sell on the market, had to be bought by the Bank at a price (and hence at an interest rate) fixed by itself. The smallness of the market for public funds and the necessity

TABLE 5.8 *Households' financial wealth (% composition)*

	1974 stocks*	*1977 stocks*	*1978 stocks*	*1982 stocks*	*1979 flows*	*1980 flows*	*1981 flows*	*1982 flows*	*1983 flows*	*1984 flows*
Banknotes and coins	8.1	6.5	6.6	5.4	4.3	5.9	5.6	3.6	3.3	2.4
Bank deposits	47.6	53.8	55.0	48.0	54.8	45.7	34.2	49.8	30.7	27.2
Postal deposits	8.4	8.7	9.2	7.1	10.2	8.0	3.2	3.8	4.0	5.2
Other deposits and ICS	3.1	2.2	2.2	3.0	1.0	0.9	2.3	9.2	1.5	3.9
Treasury bills (BOT)	–	2.9	4.0	13.4	17.6	30.5	35.9	13.8	17.5	17.6
Treasury Cred. Cert. (CCT)	–		1.7	4.6	6.3	3.0	5.4	12.4	29.1	27.7
Other m–l term bonds	13.6	9.5	8.6	4.9	0.3	–5.5	4.0	1.5	8.7	8.3
Shares	3.5	5.2	4.7	6.1	–	1.5	1.5	–	–	1.1
Foreign assets	7.9	4.4	1.1	1.0	–0.2	0.6	0.5	0.2	–	–
Other financial assets	7.8	6.8	6.8	6.5	5.6	9.5	7.3	5.7	5.3	6.3

*1974: Old series.

SOURCE: Bank of Italy, *Relazione*, various years.

of avoiding large increases in interest rates resulted, for a number of years, in the impossibility of controlling the money supply.

During the last years of the 1970s, it was instead possible to fund on the market larger and larger shares of the PSBR. Both the banks and, after a delay, the non-bank operators rapidly increased their holdings of public funds. The Bank of Italy, that in 1975 held almost 40 per cent of the total stock of public debt, was able to reduce this percentage to 23 per cent in 1979–81 and to 17.6 per cent in 1983. Having so eased the non-monetary financing of the PSBR, the way was paved for what has been called the 'divorce between the Bank of Italy and the Treasury', i.e. the repeal of the obligation to finance in monetary base the unfunded part of PSBR. The divorce came into effect gradually since July 1981. From that date on, the central bank acquired the theoretical possibility of deciding autonomously how much of the PSBR to finance through money creation.

The divorce was prepared not only by the measures taken with the aim of creating and enlarging the money markets. There was also a big change in the interest rates policy. As already mentioned, for many years the real rates remained negative, sometimes by a large amount. But, starting from the end of 1980, they became positive and significantly high: of the order of 5–6 per cent on the six-monthly Treasury bills in 1983, and still higher on other public securities.[9]

Of course, the size of the real rates was influenced by similar international evolutions. But, as an additional explanation, one has to mention the change in the intermediate objective of monetary policy. In fact, contrary to what used to happen in the past, since 1980 the growth of nominal GDP far exceeded that of money M2 (Table 5.7). The only exception is represented by the last months of 1982 when most operators refused to buy public securities because there had been rumours of a possible compulsory consolidation. Once these fears had been overcome, people resumed buying and the public sector financing was greatly eased.

In the meantime, the Bank of Italy, taking advantage of the fact that the ceiling to bank loans was no longer binding as a consequence of depression, decided to prepare its repeal and to move quickly towards the control of the money supply by *indirect* methods, i.e. through changes in the interest rates. The ceiling was lifted formally in June 1983. But up to the end of the year, the central bank exercised its moral suasion in order to maintain some control on the bank loans' expansion.

As already mentioned, the existence of the ceiling had some

undesirable consequences both because it was necessary to increase its restrictiveness and to enlarge its scope, and because it contributed to keep the interest rates to productive firms higher than would otherwise have been the case. Another, and perhaps more important, shortcoming was that the restriction of competition that it produced (by freezing the market shares of each bank) had the effect of slowing down the banks efficiency and of bringing about serious misallocations of financial resources. Hence, the repeal of the ceiling was overdue, and one has to give full credit to the Bank of Italy for having prepared well for the change and wisely supervising the problems of the transition to the new régime.

But the change from direct credit to indirect money control, while giving the Bank of Italy the possibility of choosing its targets with greater freedom and of formally separating its responsibility from that of the Treasury, has some far reaching consequences. Consider the workings of the new régime. The Bank of Italy chooses an operative target in terms of monetary base. This has the effect of fixing the level of a pivot interest rate, that on Treasury bills, which in its turn influences 'the choice of the public between deposits and government securities' and that of the banks 'between government and other securities, which determines the supply of (direct and indirect) bank credit to the private sector, for a given amount of deposits. . . . When the differential between the bank deposit rate and that on Treasury bills widens the public demand for Treasury bills increases and bank intermediation falls'.[10] The equilibrium is re-established by a rise in the interest rate on bank loans. The size of the rise depends upon the elasticity of the demand for loans. In the case of Italy, it is likely that the rise may be too large to be 'consistent with an orderly functioning of the financial and money markets'.[11]

As one can see, the implementation of a restrictive monetary policy is very difficult in the new régime. The reduction in the demand for bank loans by firms, brought about by an interest rate rise, can be far exceeded by the expansion in the PSBR due to precisely the same rise. In fact, a very large part of the outstanding public debt is represented by short-term Treasury bills and by other securities earning an interest indexed to that on Treasury bills. Therefore, any increase in the rate to be paid on the new issues of public securities will be very quickly reflected in increased interest payments on almost the whole stock of debt. It was calculated that an increase of 1 per cent in the interest rate will increase the PSBR by 2000–2500 billion lira,[12] something in the order of 0.5–0.6 per cent of the total public expenditure and 2.0–2.5 per cent of the public deficit.

Moreover, since the level of real interest rates is substantially higher than the actual and prospective real growth rates of GDP, the process of self-reproduction of the debt[13] has already started and has greatly contributed to the last few years' tremendous increase in the debt-to-GDP ratio. Keeping the real rates high means that debt accumulation is very fast and this will further increase the interest rates and reduce GDP growth.

As shown by Spaventa,[14] these gloomy results are to be expected even if the ratio of PSBR to GDP should remain constant, the proportionate rise in the interest expenditure being matched either by a corresponding increase in revenue of by a reduction in other items of expenditure. Spaventa's conclusion is: 'with a large stock of outstanding debt, a precondition to avoid unstable and potentially explosive outcomes is that fiscal policy aims at a reasonable low *f* (the ratio of the overall borrowing requirement to GDP). A desirable fiscal policy program may however prove socially and politically unfeasible unless monetary policy lends some help, . . . an austere fiscal policy program should be accompanied by a somewhat less austere attitude towards the monetary financing of the Treasury'.[15] Spaventa's warning is very clear: if the budgetary policy does not succeed in obtaining the required reduction of the PSBR to GDP ratio, a too tight monetary policy will have the effect of greatly speeding up the growth of public debt. In this way, it creates the conditions that will inevitably lead to the impossibility of funding the PSBR on the market, with the worst possible outcome: the quick monetisation of the debt in the most dramatic situation.

5.6 OVERTURNING THE RECENT GLOOMY TRENDS; PROSPECTS AND PROBLEMS

The Bank of Italy is preoccupied by the possible consequences of a too tight monetary policy. The Governor, after having stated that 'positive real interest rates are a normal characteristic of an economy growing in equilibrium', adds that 'if the real interest rate exceeds for a long time the income growth rate, the ensuing progressive increase of the debt as a ratio to output may be incompatible with the saving capacity of the economic system'. But he also says that 'a forced reduction of the interest rates would . . . be contrary to the institutional job of the central bank. This one operates with the aim of strengthening money, not of destroying it, being convinced that the healing of public finances, the resumption of growth and the reduction of inflation are possible'.[16]

The last sentence seems to be supported by the results of an exercise that tries to simulate the paths of deficits and debt for the period 1984–88, under two different sets of hypotheses.[17] The first one is given by: (1) inflation decreasing from 10 per cent in 1984 to 7 per cent in 1985 and 6 per cent thereafter; (2) real GDP growth at 3 per cent during the whole period; (3) gradual increase of 2 percentage points in the rate of taxation; (4) reduction of the real interest rate on public securities to 3 per cent starting from 1985; (5) constancy of the laws and mechanisms currently regulating public expenditure, which is estimated to imply that expenditure net of interest will grow at 4 per cent per year.

The results of the simulation are very gloomy. The ratio of PSBR to GDP will remain at the high levels (17 per cent) reached in 1983. The debt ratio to GDP will increase from 0.85 to 1.23. Notwithstanding the increased taxation and the reduced real interest rate, the possibility of avoiding the monetisation of the debt seems to be very uncertain. In fact, the market would have to hold a stock of debt that, as a ratio to GDP, would pass from 0.70 to 1.08, which is a very large increase and most unlikely to be enforceable.

The second exercise keeps unchanged the hypotheses (1) and (2), but assumes (3) an increase of 3 points in the rate of taxation; (4) a reduction of the real interest rate to 2 per cent after 1985; (5) an increase in the public expenditure net of interest of only 1 per cent. In other terms: higher taxation (1 point), lower interest rate (1 point), lower expenditure (3 points).

The results of the simulation are much brighter than in the previous case: the PSBR net of interest expenditure would fall from 6.5 per cent of GDP to 0.7 per cent; the current deficit would disappear by 1987–88; the debt to GDP ratio, after reaching a maximum of 1.02 in 1987 would slowly start to fall; the stock of debt to be held by the public would pass, as a ratio to GDP, from 0.70 to 0.85. The improvement over the previous exercise is rather impressive.

The available information on the precise formulation of the model utilised for the simulations is too scant to allow a thorough appraisal of the results. Taking them at their face value, one can say that the favourable results of the second exercise are not in sharp conflict with Spaventa's analysis. Both show that the required fiscal policy is very severe and probably cannot be achieved only by cutting expenditure.

Higher taxation seems to be unavoidable. Moreover, both consider a substantial reduction in the real interest rates as one of the ingredients of a program of public finance restoration. The difference is that there is no monetisation of the debt in the Bank of Italy's exercise, the reduction in the rate of interest coming from a reduced pressure of the PSBR on the financial markets. If it is possible to reach such a good result without increasing the money supply, all the better. But, what if it should prove impossible?

Apart from this consideration, one has to realise that the clue to the program lies in its social and political feasibility. Is it likely that the necessary increase in the rate of taxation could actually, and quickly, be obtained mainly through the reduction of tax evasion, without overburdening still more the workers and other honest tax payers? And is it possible to overcome altogether the social and political resistance to a drastic slowing down of expenditure? In view of what happened in the past, one can have one's doubts. All in all, it seems likely that the actual fiscal policy will be somewhat less severe that the one postulated in the second exercise. In this case, should the real interest rate be kept at a level higher than the postulated 2 per cent (remember that it is tax exempted)? If the degree of tightness of monetary policy remains sticky, the answer is positive. But, by so behaving, one would renounce the small, but useful, help that may come from an alternative course. With international interest rates pointing higher and higher, a policy aimed at forcing them down in Italy is clearly unsound. But, should international conditions change, it would seem unwise to discard it altogether.

5.7 POST SCRIPTUM

The above illustrated trends continued without any relevant modification in 1984 and, as far as one can judge from provisional and incomplete data, also in 1985. The PSBR, far from decreasing, seems to have reached 17.5 per cent of GDP in 1985. The ratio of public debt to GDP rose to 91.6 per cent in 1984 and to 99.7 per cent in 1985.

The monetary policy remained rather restrictive in 1984 and it was somewhat eased in 1985. The growth of M2 accelerated a little owing to a greater monetary financing of public deficit; the nominal interest rates declined in line with inflation, leaving the real rates unchanged.

During the last two months of 1985, in connection with rumours of a possible new devaluation of the lira, Italian firms started to repay external debts and to substitute them with internal ones; bank loans increased abruptly and by very large amounts. The Bank of Italy suffered a huge loss of foreign reserves. Moreover, some difficulties had been felt in funding the PSBR: it proved impossible to sell on the market the desired amount of new issues. Something had to be done.

One possible measure would have been a sharp increase in interest rates. But, owing to the already mentioned interest indexation of a large part of the debt, such a measure would have entailed a sharp increase in the public expenditure for interests. It would have been a self-defeating measure. Therefore, the Bank of Italy decided, in January 1986, to re-introduce the ceiling to the bank loans expansion that it had lifted in June 1983. This measure was announced to last only six months. Hopefully so! But one cannot help avoiding the impression that the Bank of Italy no longer has the (political) power of enforcing a highly restrictive monetary policy by pushing up the interest rates sufficiently. Direct credit controls seem to be unavoidable from time to time, with all the inefficiencies they bring about. High and continuous deficits and a rocketing debt have consequences of that kind.

NOTES

1. Bank of Italy, *Relazione del Governatore, 1983*, Rome 1984, pp. 135–6.
2. Bank of Italy, *Relazione 1983, Appendice*, pp. 34–40.
3. Bank of Italy, *Relazione 1983*, pp. 152–3.
4. M. Baldassarri, 'Spesa Pubblica e Crescita Economica', *Rivista di Politica Economica*, no. 1, 1983, pp. 77–84. See also F. Cavazzuti, *Il Nodo Della Finanza Pubblica*, (Milan: Feltrinelli, 1979).
5. Big losses are made by the public enterprises, while some of the private ones make fairly comfortable profits.
6. C. Caranza & A. Fazio, 'Methods of Monetary Control in Italy: 1974–1983', in D. R. Hodgman (ed.), *The Political Economy of Monetary Policy: National and International Aspects*, Conference series no. 26, Federal Reserve Bank of Boston, 1983, p. 67.
7. 'Total domestic credit [is] the domestic component of total financial assets (i.e. money plus short-term securities and public and private bonds) in the hands of enterprises and households; [it] consists of domestic lending to the economy (enterprises and households) plus the PSBR'. pp. 70–1.
8. Other administrative measures were utilised. Among them one should recall the 'portfolio constraint' according to which the banks were required to keep in portfolio considerable amounts of well specified bonds with the aim of channelling financial resources towards medium

term credit institutions (Instituti di credito speciale, ICS) and hence towards real investments.

9. In comparing the real interest rate on Treasury bills with that prevailing in other countries, one has to remember that in Italy the yields on the State debt are tax exempted.
10. C. Caranza & A. Fazio, pp. 84–5.
11. M. Arcelli, 'Problemi Aperti dalla Svolta di Politica monetaria', in T. Cozzi (ed.) *Moneta ed Economia Nazionale*, (Turin: Cassa di Risparmio, 1984) p. 164.
12. Ibid, p. 167.
13. See T. Sargent & N. Wallace, 'Some Unpleasant Monetarist Arithmetic', *Federal Reserve of Minneapolis Quarterly Review*, Autumn 1981.
14. See L. Spaventa, 'The Growth of Public-Debt in Italy: Past Experience, Perspectives and Policy Problems', *Banca Nazionale del Lavoro Quarterly Review*, June 1984; and also 'Nota sulla Sostenibilità della Crescita del Debito Pubblico', in T. Cozzi (ed.), *Moneta ed Economia Nazionale*.
15. Banca d'Italia, *Relazione per il 1983, Considerazioni Finali*, pp. 284–5.
17. Ibid, pp. 295–6; see also G. Morcaldo & G. Salvemini, 'Il bilancio Pubblico per il Quinquennio 1984–88: Alcune Simulazioni', *Servizio Studi della Banca d'Italia*, no. 30, July 1984.

6 Public Sector Deficits and the Growth of the National Debt

Dominique Strauss-Kahn

The very rapid growth of the internal national debt observed in most industrialised countries since the beginning of the 1970s poses questions regarding the risks of such a situation and leads one to wonder whether the advantages that are associated with the persistent public sector deficits that lie at the root of this growing indebtedness really exist.

Figures 6.1 and 6.2 show that, though there are cases of a fall in the national debt/GDP ratio (this is true of the United Kingdom, though at very high levels, of course) and though some countries have kept their ratios at a more or less constant level (such as the United States and France), in most cases gross indebtedness had doubled and net indebtedness has increased even more.

The first half of this chapter will attempt to show that it is a tricky business even to attempt to measure public sector deficits and that the exercise sometimes produces unexpected results. The second half will look at the consequences of the public sector deficits that are most usually mentioned and, in the case of France, will try to distinguish between the genuine risks and the others.

6.1 PROBLEMS OF DEFINITION AND MEASUREMENT

According to the definitions used, estimates of the budget deficit and of the national debt can vary considerably. During recent years these questions have attracted renewed interest and important work has been done with a view to making the definitions more accurate and proposing estimates.

In connection with the question of public sector debt, two observations have been made (cf. in particular Seater, 1981, Boskin, 1982, Penner, 1982, Cox & Hirschhorn, 1983 and Eisner & Pieper, 1983).

The first is that a debt which has been contracted in order to

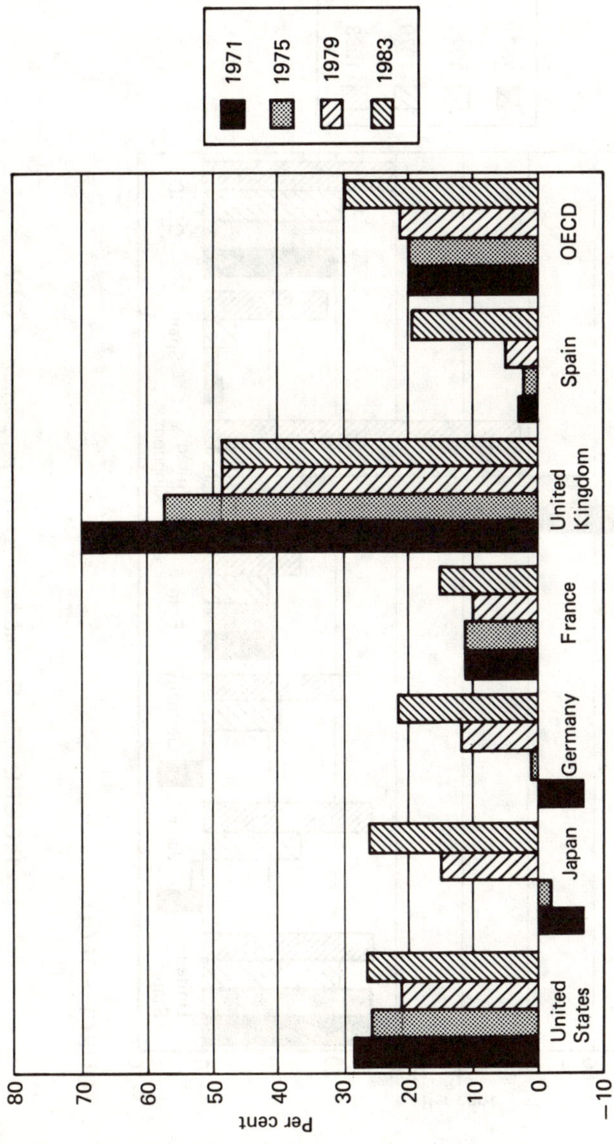

SOURCE: OECD.

FIGURE 6.1 *Gross indebtedness as a proportion of GDP*

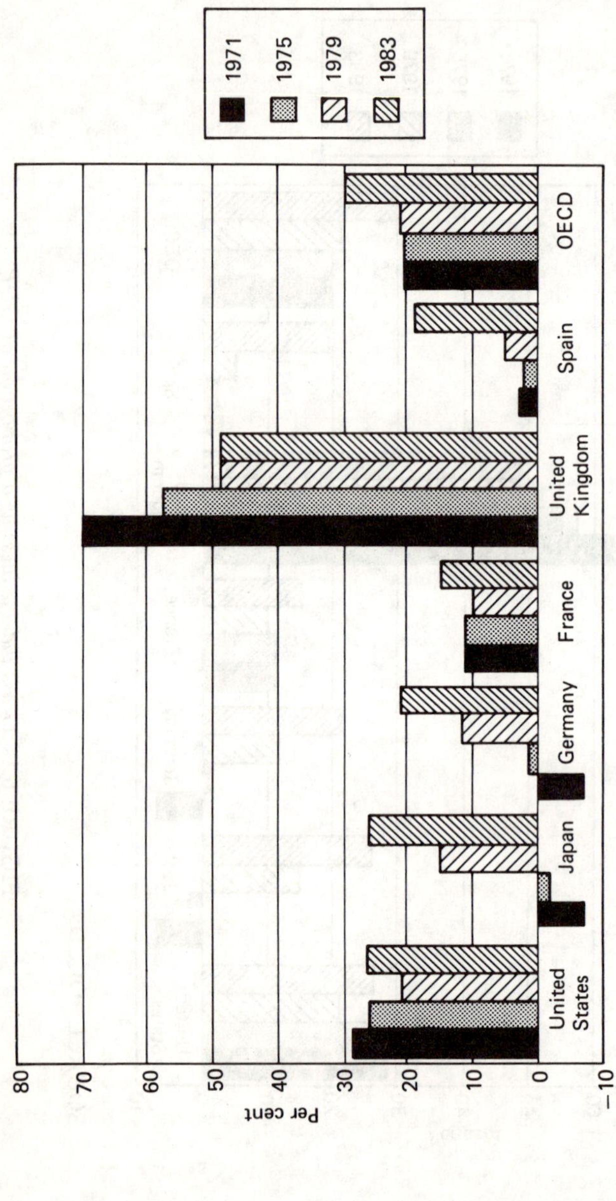

SOURCE: OECD.

FIGURE 6.2 *Net indebtedness as a proportion of GDP*

finance current expenditure cannot be looked at in the same way as a debt which has been used for capital expenditure, whether by way of direct investment by the State or investment subsidies. Incidentally, there is a degree of arbitrariness in the very definition of what constitutes capital expenditure: the expenditure incurred by the State, for example, in order to increase the available stock of human capital (expenditure on education, research etc.) may be considered a form of investment (for an argument along these lines cf. Quaden, 1982).

The second of these observations derives from the fact that inflation is most usually ignored when the value of public indebtedness is being estimated. The fact is that inflation reduces the real value of debts. Since the greater part of the national debt has been contracted at fixed interest rates, the interest payments do not make up for the fall in the real value of the capital.

The adjustments which have been made by Eisner & Pieper (1983), for example, have the effect of reducing the gross national indebtedness of the United States in 1980 from 930 000 million dollars to an estimated 447 000 million dollars. Calculations of this kind plainly show that the long-term trend of the national debt in most countries is downwards, in contrast with the widely accepted view that most countries are sinking further and further into debt.

It is also possible to calculate an inflation-adjusted budget deficit, as the OECD does (cf. Muller & Price, 1984). Adjustment for inflation reflects the fall in the real value of the national debt, corresponding to the capital losses suffered by the holders of public sector securities (see Figure 6.3): this is the way of measuring the budget deficit that is consistent with the view that sees the capital value of outstanding public sector debt falling in real terms.

It will however be noted that the inflation tax which the members of the public suffer also depends on the interest that they receive. In actual fact the inflation tax is equal to the amount of the adjustment for inflation, less net interest paid. To say that the inflation tax is positive or that the real rate of interest is negative are thus two ways of saying the same thing.

The question of whether or not we should take account of inflation for the purpose of measuring the effects of the budget deficit on demand (that is, whether we should use a balance which has been adjusted for inflation, rather than an unadjusted figure) in the end comes down to the classic problem of the influence of real wealth on households' consumption patterns. To the extent that most empirical

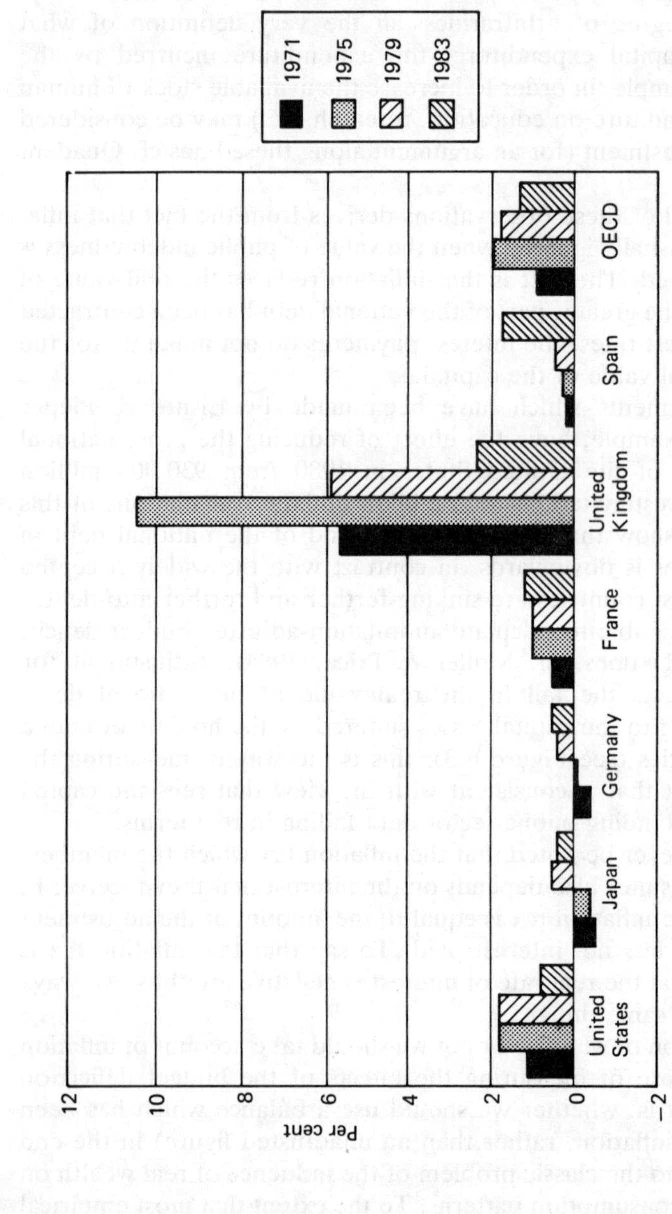

FIGURE 6.3 *Inflation adjustment/GDP*

SOURCE: OECD.

studies tend to confirm the hypothesis that real wealth has a significant influence on consumption patterns, it would seem preferable to use an inflation-adjusted balance.

Before adjusting the budget balance to allow for inflation, however, the OECD's research suggests that we should tackle another question. The fact is that the actual budget deficit as it is measured each year (see Figure 6.4) does not necessarily constitute a good indicator. Budget deficits are affected by the stage in the business cycle. They tend to be small (or even non-existent) at the highest point in the cycle and large at the bottom of the cycle. This is because the government's tax income increases as production increases whilst at the same time certain transfer payments (e.g. unemployment pay) fall. It is thus possible, using a method that has by now become traditional, to calculate an estimate of the structural budget deficit (or surplus) that corresponds to the prevailing situation at the highest point in the business cycle. Conversely, the proportion of the deficit that is due to the effect of the automatic stabilisers gradually falls as the highest point in the cycle approaches, that is, as the actual GDP and the potential GDP converge.

The structural budget deficit (Figure 6.5) is free of any effects deriving from the economic situation at the various stages in the business cycle and has two main advantages. Firstly, it can be seen to be a better indicator of the deliberate intervention of the State in the economy. In this form, the budget deficit is no longer the consequence of changes in the economic situation but is rather a cause of them. In addition, using a structural budget deficit means that it is possible to avoid the extremely pernicious consequences that would flow from any attempt to maintain a balanced budget throughout the cycle without allowing for the effects of the short-term economic situation or for the underlying structural tendencies.

Of course, this structural budget deficit will itself have to be adjusted for inflation. But before going on to make this correction, we ought to point out, following the example of Price & Muller (1984), that, in order to obtain 'measurements of the structural budget balance which are consistent with the long-term (that is, adjusted for cyclical variations) increase in the level of public-sector debt, a level of potential production must be defined, not in terms of production at the apex of the business cycle but rather in terms of the average level throughout the cycle'. We thus obtain, when all corrections have been made, the results set out in Figure 6.6.

These figures now call for some comments.

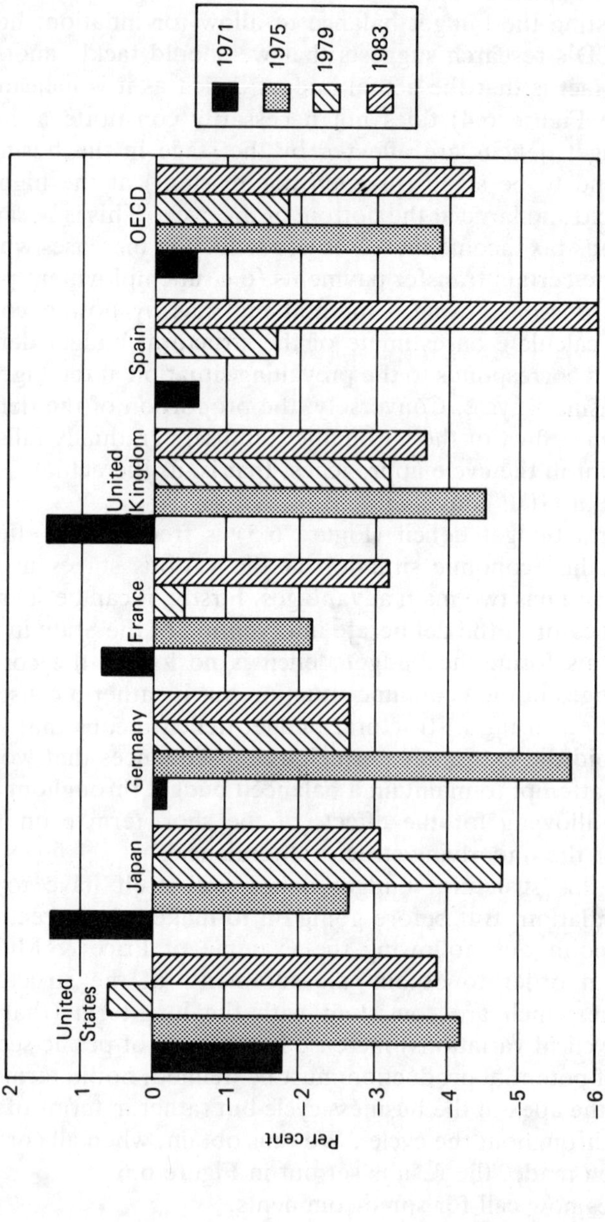

SOURCE: OECD

FIGURE 6.4 *Actual budget deficit/GDP*

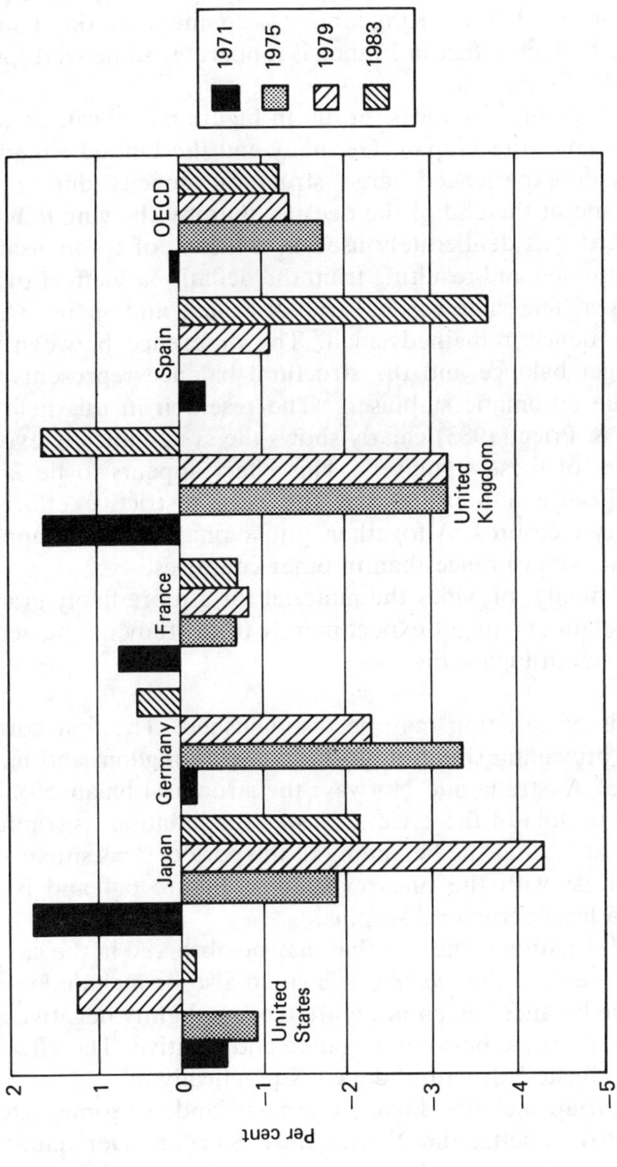

SOURCE: OECD.

FIGURE 6.5 *Structural budget deficits/GDP*

- The actual budget balances given in Figure 6.4 are very variable from one country to another and even from one year to another. It will however be observed that they are especially high in Japan, Germany or the United Kingdom, not to mention the United States. The budget deficit in France is moderate, somewhat lower than the OECD average.
- As for the structural balances set out in Figure 6.5, it can be seen that several countries (Japan, Germany and the United Kingdom in particular) experienced large structural deficits during the mid-1970s and at the end of the decade, thereby showing that the budget deficit was deliberately used as a means of compensating for the fall in demand resulting from the deflationary effect of the oil-price rises. The same was not true of France and Spain, where the budget deficit remained small. The difference between the actual budget balance and the structural balance represents the effect of the automatic stabilisers. The research in this field by Chouraqui & Price (1983) clearly shows the systematically expansionist effect of these stabilisers. This effect appears to be fairly strong in France and brings out the very restrictive effect of discretionary measures. Altogether, public finances would appear to be less active in France than in other countries.
- Figure 6.6, finally, provides the material for a more finely graded judgement than one might expect merely from studying the actual balances given in Figure 6.4.

Three kinds of situation may be distinguished. The first corresponds to the prevailing situation in the United Kingdom and might also be true of Australia and Norway: the structural balance of the budget in the middle of the cycle, adjusted for inflation, is comfortably positive, at least at the beginning of the period. This situation is in sharp contrast with the one revealed in Figure 6.4 and is the reflection of a large structural surplus.

The second situation is the one that may be observed in the case of the United States and France (Austria could also be included in this category). The balances given in Figure 6.6 are slightly negative and in some cases alternate between negative and positive. The effect of the inflation-adjusted structural deficit is practically nil.

The third group includes Japan, Germany and, to some extent, Spain (and also Canada, the Netherlands, Sweden, Denmark and Ireland). In these countries the budget deficit appears to have been used as a means of propping up demand. It can thus be seen that it is

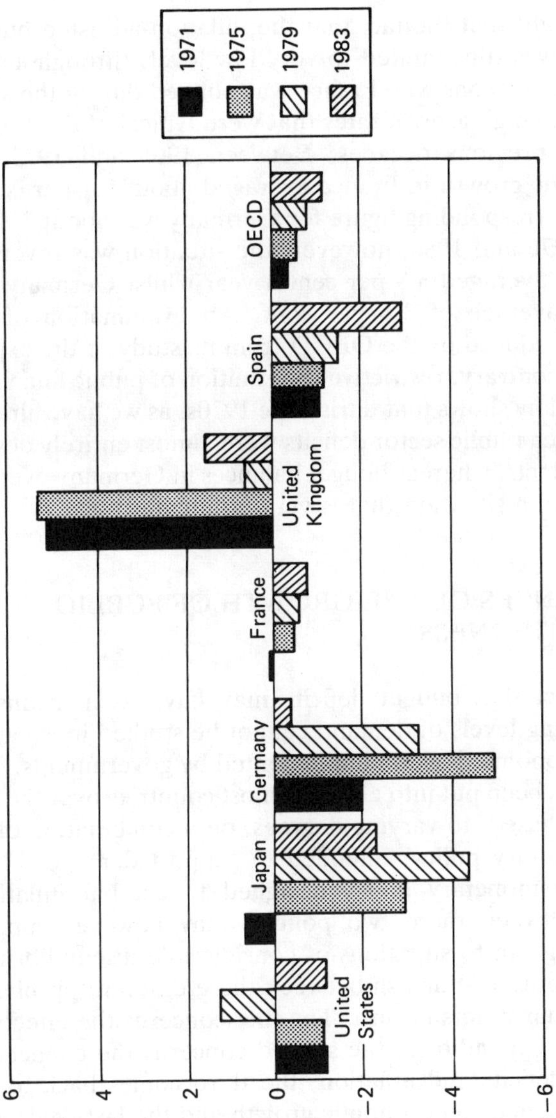

SOURCE: OECD.

FIGURE 6.6 *Structural budget deficits adjusted for inflation in mid-cycle/GDP*

not always the countries that are accused of the greatest 'laxity' in budgetary matters which are actually guilty of deliberately cultivating large budget deficits.

It may be thought that the fact that the inflation-adjusted budget deficit in France was thus limited to very low levels throughout the 1970s is one of the reasons why France was obliged during the same period to forgo the high growth rates that were typical of the French economy during previous decades. Between 1961 and 1975, for example, economic growth in France averaged about 5.1 per cent a year, whilst the corresponding figure for Germany was about 3.8 per cent. Between 1976 and 1980, however, the situation was reversed: growth in France averaged 3.3 per cent a year whilst Germany was notching up an average of 3.6 per cent. An examination of the detailed results produced by the OECD from its study of the expansionist or, on the contrary, restrictive, orientation of public finance in France and Germany shows that during the 1970s, as we have already pointed out, French public sector deficits were almost entirely devoid of expansionist effects, whereas budget balances in Germany over the same period reveal a situation that is very 'graduated'.

6.2 CONSEQUENCES OF THE GROWTH OF PUBLIC SECTOR INDEBTEDNESS

The positive effect that budget deficits may have as a means of propping up sagging levels of demand cannot be studied in isolation from the other economic policies implemented by governments. The policy mix that has been put into effect by most countries over the last ten years or so is based, to varying degrees, on a combination of an expansionist budgetary policy, intended to support demand, along with a restrictive monetary policy designed to combat inflation. Contradictions between these two policies may however appear, leading in the long run to situations of considerable disequilibrium. In order to attempt to distinguish between these different problems, we shall look at four points in turn. The first concerns the effectiveness of budgetary expenditure, the second concerns the connection between budget deficits and inflation, the third comes back to the effects of budget deficits on economic growth and the last deals with the effect of budget deficits on the savings rate.

1. The growth of public sector debt resulting from accumulated budget deficits poses an initial problem connected with the structure

of the budget. The fact is that this growth of public sector debt results in higher and higher interest payments (cf. Figure 6.7). Interest payments of this kind, as a percentage of GDP, more than doubled in the OECD countries during the period 1971–83: in Japan they rose eightfold and in Germany they tripled.

Two consequences must be noted. The first is that the ever-growing share of government expenditure taken up by public sector debt service proportionately reduces the amount of other expenditure, assuming that tax revenue and budget deficits remain the same. The effectiveness of public expenditure is thus inhibited, unless the government is prepared to allow the deficit to rise even further, which will itself result in even higher interest payments. This cumulative effect, which is of course even harder to control when interest rates are high (e.g. as a result of a restrictive monetary policy), is one of the most serious dangers inherent in the growth of public sector indebtedness. It is not hard to imagine a situation when, faced with the political impossibility of raising taxes or of reducing expenditure, a government finds that there is no other way out of the dilemma but to accept higher inflation in order to have the benefit of the resulting reduction in the real value of its debts (cf. Larosière, 1984).

The second consequence concerns the question of equity. It has often been pointed out that the high level of interest rates that has prevailed for some years now amounts to an act of historic revenge-taking by lenders over borrowers. However, though it is reasonable for a borrower to accept high rates of interest on his borrowings in line with the handsome profits he expects to make, the situation is not quite the same when the borrower is the State. In that case the interest payments will be met by the taxpayer, the actual, though unconsulted, borrower, and the growth of the debt results in considerable 'reverse' redistribution of income.

2. Analysis of the links between budget deficits and inflation is a delicate matter. It is often claimed that public sector deficits are by their very nature always inflationary. Two main reasons are usually cited:

- By increasing demand, the budget deficit applies pressure to inadequate productive capacities and a rise in prices is the result of the renewed tension on the markets;
- Because budget deficits are often at least partly financed by monetary creation, they result in an injection of new money into the economy which has a pernicious effect on prices; in cases where the

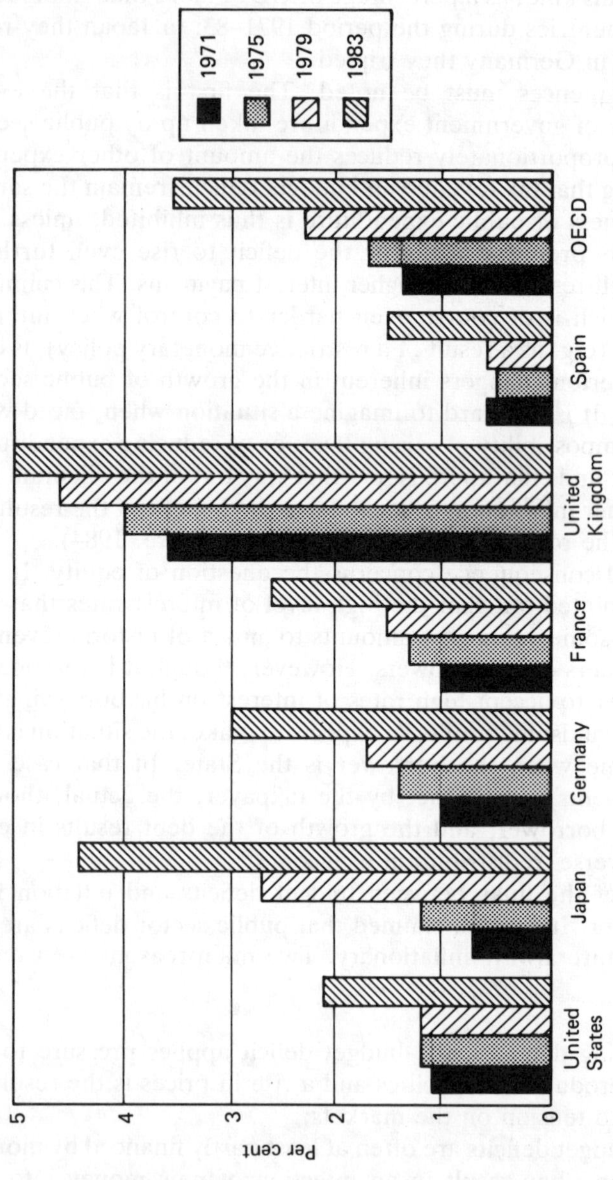

FIGURE 6.7 *Interest paid/GDP*

SOURCE: OECD.

deficit is mainly financed by borrowing, this effect on the price level does not apply (or applies to only a limited extent) but the crowding out of private companies from the capital markets has in the end a comparable effect thanks to the rise in interest rates.

This very sweeping kind of reasoning is no doubt in need of some qualification. First of all, the answer to the question of whether or not the extra demand is the cause of inflationary pressures mainly depends on the state of the productive system. To some extent, public sector deficits, by guaranteeing a minimum level of demand and by regulating it, may even be anti-inflationary, because they make it possible for companies to spread their fixed costs over a greater volume of production. In the medium term, everything depends on the effect of the deficit on the restructuring of the supply of goods and services. If the deficit is the result of considerable expenditure by the State with a view to facilitating the introduction of new technologies or reorganising production in a particular industrial sector, it may in the medium term have very positive effects on production capacities and costs and by so doing it will help to reduce inflationary tensions.

As for the question of whether or not public sector deficits are more or less inflationary according to the way they are financed, the answer broadly depends on the way the financial system of the country works and on the type of monetary regulation adopted. According to the type of financing and the system of monetary regulation (more or less active interdependence of the counterparts to the money supply), the deficit will authorise a greater or smaller supply of credit, and that will reinforce or weaken the expansionist effect of the increase in public spending; this does not however imply any *a priori* conclusions regarding the distribution of the increase in demand as between production and prices. Financing by monetary creation will thus have more important effects on economic activity than financing by an issue of bonds but the increase in the activity/inflationary effect ratio may well be about the same (cf. Sterdyniak, 1982, 1983).

Everything depends on the exchange rate system involved. In a system of fixed exchange rates it may be argued that financing by monetary creation is less inflationary than financing by a bond issue because it helps to keep interest rates down. In the short term, therefore, financing by monetary creation produces lower financial charges for companies. Conversely, in a system of floating rates, financing by a bond issue may be less inflationary than financing by monetary creation. The fact is that in a system of floating rates the parity of the currency changes in inverse proportion to the inflation rate and in direct proportion to the interest rate. The exchange rate will therefore be all the lower if interest rates are low. Now, empirical studies show that the effect of a fall in currency parities on prices is greater than that of a variation in interest rates.

Observation of the trend of the money supply cannot very easily be used as an indicator for judging the effects of the various types of financing on the supply of credit, especially when, as is the case in France, monetary regulation is based on quantitative controls. What is more, the financial innovations introduced in recent years are such as to make the distinction between monetary and non-monetary assets more and more blurred.

It should be noted, finally, that an IMF study of 1982 demonstrated the lack of connection, in most countries, between the growth of the public sector deficit and inflation, and in those cases where a significant connection could be established the causality was most usually reversed.

3. Some doubt has been cast on the effectiveness of budget deficits as devices for maintaining the level of demand because of the various crowding out effects that may appear. The basic line of argument is as follows. If the volume of private investment and consumption which would have existed in the absence of the deficit is reduced by the effects of the deficit there is no guarantee that overall demand will increase and it may even fall. We shall look here at the question of financial crowding out, and more particularly crowding out in connection with economic agents' preferences for money or securities.

An increase in subscriptions to government loans intended to finance the budget deficit without recourse to monetary creation may be the result of a fall in demand for private sector bonds. In that case the result is certainly a crowding out of private spending by public spending. But these extra subscriptions may also reflect a fall in economic agents' holdings of liquid assets. In this case there will be no crowding out effect if, in spite of a lower level of holdings of liquid assets, private sector demand remains unchanged. This will depend both on the interest-rate elasticity of the demand for money and on the interest-rate elasticity of private sector demand (consumption and investment). If the former elasticity is strong and the latter weak, the crowding out effect will be minimal. The experience of France in recent years rather tends to support this view, though it is very difficult to estimate these elasticities consistently. In response to the rise in interest rates which was connected with both the international economic situation, the Government's desire to develop the French financial markets and the pressure of increasing public sector borrowings, considerable quantities of savings have abandoned liquid forms of assets in favour of long-term securities, thereby evidencing a fairly strong elasticity. Conversely, the influence of small variations in interest rates on investment decisions seems to be practically nil, which is why it is reasonable to think that there has been practically no crowding out of this kind in France in recent years.

As for crowding out in connection with portfolio effects, due to excessively high concentrations of government securities amongst economic agents' portfolio assets (which thus cause a rise in interest rates in order to ensure continuing ease of placement of government securities), such a form of crowding out is by its very nature difficult to measure. However, it does not appear that the share of the financial markets taken by the State in France today is considered excessive by those who lend on these markets.

All the same, there is another form of crowding out that could be mentioned. In a country where the demand for credit is rationed, crowding out may manifest itself otherwise than through high interest rates. The fall in balances of liquid assets took the form in France of withdrawals from demand deposit accounts and from savings accounts for house purchases. To the extent that such deposits on the one hand confer the right to a housing loan and on the other are a source of refinancing for the mortgage market, the transfer of considerable sums to the financial markets may limit the quantities available for investment in housing even supposing that demand remains strong, that is, even if the yields expected on the housing market continue to be high. The existence of numerous 'circuits' in the place of 'markets' then encourages a form of 'institutional crowding out', the proportions of which are not, however, easy to measure.

4. One last question concerns the effect of the budget deficit on national savings. As Figure 6.8 shows, the ratio between the public sector deficit and net private savings is tending to increase. For some years now there has been a return in economic literature to the hypothesis of the rational expectations of economic agents, and especially of households. (For a review of the literature, cf. Buiter & Tobin, 1979 and Holcombe, Jackson & Zardkoohi, 1981.) According to this hypothesis and in the case of the national debt, households act in anticipation of the subsequent rise in taxes which will be needed in order to repay the debt, that is, they limit their consumption so as to

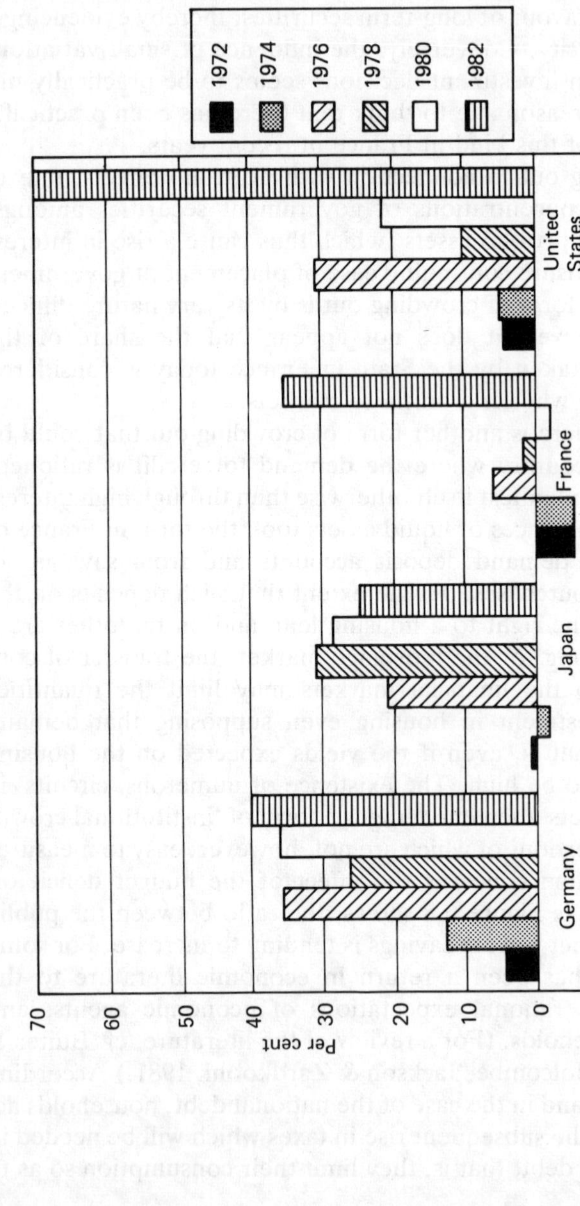

SOURCE: IMF.

FIGURE 6.8 *Public sector deficit/net private savings*

accumulate the resources they will need to pay future taxes. This being so, modifying macroeconomic equilibria using the budget deficit becomes impossible. As is well known, this proposition, which was given renewed currency by Barro (1974), is based on a series of hypotheses which are, to say the least, very far-reaching: apart from the fact that households are assumed to be able to make very precise forecasts, we also have to assume that the capital market is perfect and transfers of information from one generation to another are such as to make economic agents' ability to look forwards into the future and backwards into the past almost infinite. A theoretical criticism and some empirical estimates of these various points in the case of France have been proposed by Kessler, Masson and Strauss-Kahn (1979) in connection with the question of the link between savings and the social security system.

In Strauss-Kahn (1983) some new estimates are suggested which clarify the national debt using both Kochin's model and that of Buiter and Tobin. Kochin's model is one of the first to have been used. In the case of the United States, the estimates obtained seem to indicate that a deficit of 100 implies a reduction in consumption of 11. It would thus appear that there is some partial expectation of future taxes. Using quarterly data for France, the results are somewhat different. In fact, the variable that represents the budget deficit is never significant and the variation of the monetary base is a negative one. As for Buiter and Tobin's models, they are based on a comparison between one equation, which includes, separately, income, fiscal pressure and the budget deficit, and another which includes only one variable: income – taxes + public spending. The American, French and Belgian results tend to the same conclusion in this respect: the coefficient associated with indebtedness is not significant and it may be concluded that use of debt funding does not have the same effects as taxes on savings.

In spite of the fact that the test used is an extremely rough one, the results in the case of France suggest that the hypothesis of equivalence should be rejected. Koskela & Viren (1983) have come to a similar conclusion regarding nine OECD countries which they studied over the period 1964–79.

This chapter has tried to show that the effects of budget deficits on demand cannot be established as rapidly as people often suggest. Thanks to the OECD'S researches, it can be seen that, far from being in deficit, some countries evince structural surpluses.

Furthermore, the second half of this study has tried to demonstrate that the risks which are conventionally supposed to accompany public sector deficits (such as crowding out, negative effects on savings and inflation) do not appear, in the case of France, to be the most important ones: what seemed to give cause for concern is rather more the cumulative effect of servicing the debt and the resulting reduction of the government's margin of manoeuvre.

REFERENCES

Barro R. J. (1974) 'Are Government Bonds Net Wealth?' *Journal of Political Economy*, 1974, **6**, pp. 1095–117.

Boskin M. J. (1982) 'Federal Government Deficits: Some Myths and Realities', *American Economic Review*, May 1982, **72**, pp. 296–303.

Buiter W. & Tobin J. (1979) 'Debt Neutrality: a Brief Review of Doctrine and Evidence', in *Social Security Versus Private Saving*, G. Von Furstenberg (ed.), Ballinger Publishing Co., 1977, pp. 39–63.

Chouraqui J. C. & Price R. (1983) 'Les Déficits du Secteur Public: Problèmes et Implications en Matière de Politique Économique' OCDE, *Etudes Spéciales*, June 1983.

Cox M. & Hirschhorn E. (1983) 'The Market Value of US Government Debt: Monthly, 1942–1980', *Journal of Monetary Economics*, March 1983, **1**, pp. 261/272.

Eisner R. & Pieper P. J. (1983) 'A New View of the Federal Debt and Budget Deficits', Northeastern University & University of Illinois, June 1983.

Holcombe R. G., Jackson J. D. & Zardkoohi A. (1981) 'The National Debt Controversy' *Kyklos*, 1981, **2**, pp. 186–202.

Kessler D., Masson A. & Strauss-Kahn D. (1979) 'Epargne et Prévoyance Collective', *Organisation des Nations-Unies*, 1979.

Kochin L. A. (1974) 'Are Future Taxes Anticipated by Consumers?', *Journal of Money, Credit and Banking*, 1974, **3**, pp. 385–94.

Koskela E. & Viren M. (1983) 'National Debt Neutrality: Some International Evidence', Kyklos, vol. 36, fasc. 4, 1983.

Larosiere J. de (1984) 'La Croissance de la Dette Publique et L'exigence de Discipline Financière', *40è Congrès des IIFP*, Innsbruck, Aug. 1984.

Muller P. & Price W. R. (1984) 'Déficits Budgétaires Structurels et Orientations de la Politique Budgétaire', Document de Travail, *OCDE*, July 1984.

Penner R. G. (1982) 'How Much is Owed by the Federal Government?' in *Monetary Economic Review*, May 1981, **71**, pp. 134–8.

Quaden G. (1982) 'L'Expérience Belge des Déficits Publics' Colloque du Groupe de Réflexion Economiques et Financières, Paris, 09.11.82, in *Problèmes Economiques* 23.02.83, **1812**, pp. 29–32.

Seater J. J. (1981) 'The Market Value of Outstanding Government Debt 1919–1975', *Journal of Monetary Economics*, 1981, **8**, pp. 85–101.

Sterdyniak H. (1982) 'Financement Monétaire, Financement Obligataire des Déficits Publics', *Observatoire Français des Conjonctures Economiques*, note ronéotée, Sept. 1982.

Sterdyniak H. (1983) 'Théories et Pratiques du Déficit Public', *Observations et Diagnostics Économiques*, **3**, Feb. 1983.

Strauss-Kahn D. (1983) 'Un Réexamen de Quelques Questions Traditionnelles Appliqué au Cas des Déficits Publics en France,' *SUERF*, Madrid, Oct. 1983.

Index